Thomas N. Garavan · Fergal O'Brien ·
James Duggan · Claire Gubbins ·
Yanqing Lai · Ronan Carbery ·
Sinead Heneghan · Ronnie Lannon ·
Maura Sheehan · Kirsteen Grant

Learning and Development Effectiveness in Organisations

An Integrated Systems-Informed Model of Effectiveness

palgrave
macmillan

Thomas N. Garavan
School of Business
National College of Ireland
Dublin, Ireland

Fergal O'Brien
Graduate & Professional Studies
University of Limerick
Limerick, Ireland

James Duggan
Cork University Business School
University College Cork
Cork, Ireland

Claire Gubbins
DCU Business School
Dublin City University
Dublin, Ireland

Yanqing Lai
Business School
Manchester Metropolitan University
Manchester, UK

Ronan Carbery
Cork University Business School
University College Cork
Cork, Ireland

Sinead Heneghan
Irish Institute of Training and Development
Naas, Ireland

Ronnie Lannon
The Business School
Edinburgh Napier University
Edinburgh, UK

Maura Sheehan
The Business School
Edinburgh Napier University
Edinburgh, UK

Kirsteen Grant
The Business School
Edinburgh Napier University
Edinburgh, UK

ISBN 978-3-030-48902-1 ISBN 978-3-030-48900-7 (eBook)
https://doi.org/10.1007/978-3-030-48900-7

This Palgrave Macmillan imprint is published by the registered company Springer Nature Switzerland AG
The registered company address is: Gewerbestrasse 11, 6330 Cham, Switzerland

Learning and Development Effectiveness in Organisations

"Learning and Development in Organizations provides a compelling integration of research, scholarship and organisational practice in the emergent field of Learning and Development. Across its five chapters, this work provides expert insight into the contribution of learning and development for individual employability and career advancement, and for organisational sustainability and competitive advantage. The authors represent an impressive range of research, teaching and practitioner excellence. Their monograph provides a much-needed go-to resource for those whose interest is in learning and development as a feature of organisational effectiveness."

—Valerie Anderson, *Professor of Human Resource Development, University of Portsmouth, UK*

"Thomas Garavan and his colleagues have produced an exemplary analysis of what we need to know so that training delivers results. Covering all aspects of the training process, this book offers an in-depth guide to the latest research with clear practical implications drawn out. This is essential reading for anyone with a passionate interest in getting training right and wanting greater returns from their training budget."

—Professor Nicholas Clarke, *Professor of Organisational Behaviour and HRM, Loughborough University*

"At last, we have a resource that integrates research and practice written by eminent scholars. This critical view of common practices, informed by extensive theories will help both researchers and practitioners to avoid the traps of fads that have been present in L&D for many years, enabling organisations to use L&D more effectively to accomplish many outcomes desired. This is a must-read book for anyone researching or practicing L&D. The need for such knowledge will expand exponentially as we work to re-establish business following the Covid-19 Virus Pandemic."

—Gary N. McLean, *Professor of Organization Development, School of Management, Assumption University, Bangkok, Thailand*

"Assessing the effects and value of investment in training has been of continuing concern to training professionals for many years. This is not only because of their desire to provide effective interventions for the benefit of learners, but also because of the need to demonstrate value to organisation decision makers. This new text from Professor Garavan and his colleagues provides the latest and most exemplary answer to this concern through a comprehensive and thorough analysis of current research and knowledge. The result is a process model of training effectiveness which specifies all of the direct and indirect variables influencing training effectiveness. The model is clearly explained and justified in the book, and it will be of immeasurable benefit to both researchers and professionals seeking to understand how to ensure the effectiveness of training interventions."

—Professor Jim Stewart, *Liverpool Business School, Liverpool John Moores University, UK*

Contents

About the Authors

Thomas N. Garavan is a Professor of Leadership Practice at University College Cork and Visiting Research Professor, National College of Ireland, Dublin, and is a Leading Researcher worldwide in learning and development, HRD, leadership development and workplace learning. He graduated from the University of Limerick, Ireland, with a Bachelor of Business Studies and completed a Doctorate of Education at the University of Bristol. He is Editor of the European Journal of Training and Development and Associate Editor of Personnel Review. He is a member of the Editorial Board of Human Resource Management Journal, Human Resource Development Quarterly, Human Resource Development Review, Advances in Developing Human Resources, and Human Resource Development International. He is the recipient of the Academy of Human Resource Development, Outstanding HRD Scholar Award 2013. His research interests include CSR and transformational leadership, cross-cultural dimensions of diversity training, tacit knowledge in manufacturing, international human resource management standards and human resource management.

Fergal O'Brien is Assistant Dean of Graduate & Professional Studies at the University of Limerick and Senior Lecturer in Finance at the Kemmy Business School. He holds a Ph.D. in Finance from Lancaster University. Dr. O'Brien is currently working on a number of research projects including the role of tacit knowledge in organisations and risk management strategies in agriculture. He has been recognised for his teaching by being awarded the Jennifer Burke Award for Innovation in Teaching and Learning as part of the University of Limerick team. Dr. O'Brien is a board member of the World Sports Team.

James Duggan is a Ph.D. Scholar at the Cork University Business School, University College Cork, Ireland. With a background in new media and technology, James' research examines the changing nature of HRM and employment relations in the future workplace. In particular, his research focuses on algorithmic management practices and the fragmented nature of working relationships in app-based work in the global gig economy. James' Ph.D. research is funded by the Irish Research Council, having been awarded the prestigious Government of Ireland Postgraduate Scholarship to complete his studies.

Claire Gubbins is Senior Lecturer of Organisational Behaviour & HRM at DCU, Director of DCU's Executive MBA Programme, Associate Editor for Human Resource Development Quarterly (an SSCI listed journal) and Deputy Director of LINK Research Institute (Knowledge and Learning). Claire was also a Fulbright Scholar at Carnegie Mellon University USA, Senior Research Fellow on the Irish Centre for Manufacturing Research (ICMR) project on Tacit Knowledge Management, Learning and Systems, and a Senior Research Fellow at the Enterprise Research Centre with the University of Limerick. She received the DCU Presidents award for Excellence in Teaching (Assessment & feedback) in 2013.

Yanqing Lai is Senior Lecturer in HRM/HRD at Manchester Metropolitan Business School. Previously, she was a Research Assistant in Leadership/HRM in Edinburgh Napier Business School. She received her Ph.D. in Business Management from Kingston University

London in 2016, M.Sc. in Accounting and Finance from the University of Manchester (2009–2010) and B.A. (Hons.) in International Business Management from the University of Nottingham (2005–2009). Her primary research interests include strategic human resource management, subjective employee well-being and strategy and growth in entrepreneurial SMEs. Her work has been published in top-tier business and management journals, including the Journal of Business Venturing, International Small Business Management and Human Resource Management Review.

Ronan Carbery is Co-Director of the Human Resource Research Centre in UCC and lectures and researches in a variety of Human Resource Management and Human Resource Development subjects in the School of Management and Marketing. His research interests include learning and development, career development and talent management. Ronan worked at the University of Limerick from 2007 to 2014 and was awarded the Teaching Excellence award there in 2013. He is an External Examiner at Coventry University, Ulster University, Waterford Institute of Technology and London South Bank University. Ronan has co-edited a number of leading international texts and is Co-Editor of the European Journal of Training and Development.

Sinead Heneghan has worked in senior roles with the Irish Institute of Training & Development for over 18 years. In her capacity of CEO, she leads the team to develop a high value member offer and the strategic alliance of the IITD with all stakeholders. Sinead has vast experience with Individuals, Corporates, Further and Higher Education Providers and State Agencies and has represented the industry in an influencing and advocacy role for many years. She has an M.Sc. in Leadership & Change Management, a B.A. in Local and Community Development and a Certificate in Training & Development. She served as a board member of IFTDO (International Federation of Training & Development Organisations) which represents more than 500,000 learning and development professionals in over 30 countries. Sinead volunteers with the Kildare Branch of Down Syndrome Ireland where she manages a specialist Speech & Language Therapy Service for 70 people with Down Syndrome.

Ronnie Lannon has extensive teaching experience at undergraduate and postgraduate levels. He completed a research degree in the strategic management of new technology in the banking sector and subsequently worked in a strategic planning capacity in local government before returning to teach strategic management at Edinburgh Napier University Business School. Ronnie has undertaken a range of programme leadership and teaching and learning activities within The Business School. He has extensive admissions and student recruitment experience having developed articulation arrangements for both international and domestic advanced entry students. He was recently confirmed as the Business School Academic Lead for Quality Enhancement. He has also undertaken a range of Examiner roles and is currently an External Examiner for the Bachelor of Business Administration (Honours) programme at Tunku Abdul Rahman University College, Malaysia.

Maura Sheehan is Professor of International Management, specialising in HRM, HRD and organisational performance. Maura's work appears in journals such as British Journal of Industrial Relations; Cambridge Journal of Economics; Industrial and Corporate Change; International Journal of Human Resource Management; International Small Business Journal; Personnel Psychology. Before coming to Edinburgh Napier, Maura was a Professor at the National University of Ireland (NUI) Galway. Previous to this, she was a Reader at the University of Brighton and an Associate Professor at the Graduate School of Management, University of Dallas. Maura has a B.Sc. in Economics from New York University and a Ph.D. in Economics from the University of Notre Dame, USA.

Kirsteen Grant is Associate Professor (Work and Employment) and Deputy Head of Research in the Business School at Edinburgh Napier University. Kirsteen draws on complementary backgrounds in academia and organisational practice. Her research interests centre around: professional, responsible and precarious work; future of work; younger workers;

organisational leadership; talent management; workplace skills utilisation. Kirsteen co-convenes the Work and Equalities in Society research group within the university, and she is Editor of the Journal of Management Development (Emerald). Kirsteen is a Chartered Fellow of the CIPD, Senior Fellow of the HEA and Certified Management and Business Educator (CMBE).

List of Figures

List of Tables

1
Introduction

Abstract Scholars and practitioners both acknowledge the important role that learning and development (L&D) plays in organisations. The development of human capital is an essential component of individual employability, career advancement and competitive advantage. Therefore, the development of the knowledge, skills and attitudes of employees constitutes a very important organisational HR practice and it is viewed as one of the most important HR challenges that organisations face. Accordingly, the evidence indicates that organisations continue to invest in L&D programmes as part of their HR strategy. There has been an enormous expansion of research on L&D in organisations; however, a certain degree of ambiguity exists concerning the effectiveness of these activities and there is limited understanding about the best way to implement them. This finding was, for us, an important reason to write this monograph. We seek to offer an integrated and contextualised framework for L&D effectiveness which addresses both the nature of L&D and its antecedents and outcomes in organisations. We created our L&D effectiveness model based on key findings from reviews, empirical research and meta-analyses as well as from previous established theoretical frameworks within the field. We set out in this monograph to bridge

T. N. Garavan et al.
Learning and Development Effectiveness in Organisations,
https://doi.org/10.1007/978-3-030-48900-7_1

theory and practice so that our framework guides L&D researchers in their future research efforts and helps practitioners in their L&D activities.

Keywords Learning and development in organisations · Effectiveness · Integrated model

For more than four decades, learning and development (L&D) is a critical agenda issue for senior managers in organisations (Garavan et al. 2020a). There is an important recognition that organisations require a skilled and motivated workforce in order to achieve firm performance and competitive advantage (Hughes et al 2019; Tharenou et al 2007). Through investment in structured and formal L&D, organisations enhance employee and organisational human capital which leads to enhanced performance (Jiang et al 2012).

For the purpose of this monograph, we define L&D effectiveness as the extent to which it leads to intended firm-level performance gains and results. However, we also acknowledge consistent with Kirkpatrick (1987) that L&D also leads to more proximal outcomes such as feelings and reactions about the activities, enhanced knowledge, skills and abilities and learnings for teams and organisations, including HR outcomes such as job satisfaction, employee engagement and lower levels of absenteeism (Sitzmann et al. 2008; Kraiger et al. 1993). However, the ultimate outcomes that firms expect from investment in L&D are outcomes such as productivity, innovation, customer service and financial performance (Garavan et al. 2020a; Ployhart and Hale 2014). Therefore, for L&D to be effective, it is necessary to have a high degree of transfer in the form of job performance.

Despite the popularity of L&D in both research and practice, there is a great deal yet to know about the effectiveness of these practices. The lack of compelling evidence for the effectiveness of L&D (defined as 'formal on- and off-the-job structured activities focused on the development of the knowledge, skills and abilities (KSAs) for current and future job roles' (Garavan et al. 2020a: 2), has heightened recent debates about whether L&D is a worthy and valuable investment for organisations. Addressing these sorts of issues, as well as reaching consensus about L&D research and practice in general requires an evaluation of where we are at this time. This is the primary purpose of this monograph, which identifies a pressing need based on an extensive review of the L&D effectiveness literature. We provide a theoretically grounded, comprehensive and integrated framework to understand L&D and its outcomes for organisations.

We propose that there is a need for this framework based on recent discussions. For example, Garavan et al. (2019) questioned whether sufficient empirical attention has been given to justifying the contribution of L&D to firm performance in organisations. Similarly, there has been a push to justify L&D as an important strategic activity in organisations (Garavan et al. 2020b). More generally, commentators have highlighted that there is a need to improve the research base to establish the impact of L&D practices and the justification of many of the normative best practice recommendations that are found in the L&D literature (Garavan et al. 2020b). An important challenge concerns the many different ways in which 'value', 'impact', 'return' and 'bottom line' are defined and what they mean in the context of L&D. Researchers have historically argued for different dimensions of value including human resource outcomes (Tharenou et al. 2007), operational outcomes (Garavan et al. 2020a) and financial outcomes (Garavan et al. 2020b). For example, a proximal outcome perspective emphasises KSAs, cognitive, affective and behavioural outcomes (Tharenou et al. 2007); a distal perspective on the other hand argues that investment in L&D is a vehicle to improve operational and financial firm performance. This strategic view prioritises financial outcomes and argues that profitability and return on equity (ROE) represent the ultimate criterion (Kim and Ployhart 2014; Garavan et al. 2020b).

Relatively few models exist that explain the factors that are relevant to explaining the effectiveness of L&D in organisations (Garavan (2007) is perhaps one example). In response, as part of this monograph, we created a comprehensive theoretical model to understand L&D effectiveness. This model is derived from a combination of theoretical and empirical work conducted to date. Therefore, the creation of a comprehensive model is our primary contribution and represents a significant step forward on prior work in a number of important ways. First, we integrate the findings from both research and practice, which is considered a longstanding gap in the literature. We seek to integrate theoretical perspectives and both macro environmental and micro organisational factors to understand L&D effectiveness. We argue that to better understand the effectiveness of L&D, it is necessary to incorporate external and internal macro and micro level constructs in addition to understanding the roles of L&D processes in linking them to firm performance outcomes. We are therefore able to more clearly articulate how various external and internal contingencies are linked, in addition to understanding the various dynamics that underpin the effectiveness of L&D in organisations.

Our model (Fig. 4.1) has important implications for both research and practice. We first of all believe that it provides a valuable contribution in directing future research and to identify implications for researchers. Second, regarding implications for practice, the integration of existing research will point to the important dimensions of L&D that will make the biggest differences to its effectiveness in organisations. Therefore, this enables organisations and L&D practitioners interested in deriving firm performance outcomes to understand which practices, structures and levers are likely to be most impactful. We clearly specify the most important proximal and distal outcomes that can be derived from investment in L&D. The distal outcomes are often viewed as the most important; however, there are important proximal outcomes that directly link to distal outcomes. Third, we argue that our model has a contribution to make to the strategic L&D literature, which has for some time highlighted the need to better understand the 'black box' linking L&D investment to firm performance (Messersmith et al. 2011).

In the sections that follow we first provide an overview of the evolution of L&D and the forces for change that will shape its future evolution. We then describe in detail the key components of our model, drawing on the existing research base. We then consider the future choices that will help the L&D function to both evolve and transform. The final section of the monograph further elaborates on the research and practice implications and identifies the most pressing future research questions, as well as identifying what may work best in practice.

References

ATD—Association for Talent Development. (2019). *Talent development salary and benefits report*. Available from https://www.td.org/atd-research.

Hughes, A., Zajac, S., Woods, A. L., & Salas, E. (2019). The role of work environment in training sustainment: A meta-analysis. *Human Factors, 62,* 1–18.

Jiang, J., Wang, S., & Zhao, S. (2012). Does HRM facilitate employee creativity and organizational innovation? A study of Chinese firms. *International Journal of Human Resource Management, 23*(19), 4025–4047.

Garavan, T. N. (2007). A strategic perspective on human resource development. *Advances in Developing Human Resources, 9*(1), 11–30.

Garavan, T. N., Heneghan, S., O'Brien, F., Gubbins, C., Lai, Y., Carbery, R. et al. (2019). L&D professionals in organisations: Much ambition, unfulfilled promise. *European Journal of Training & Development, 44*(1), 1–86.

Garavan, T., McCarthy, A., Lai, Y., Murphy, K., Sheehan, M., & Carbery, R. (2020a). Training and organisational performance: A meta-analysis of temporal, institutional, and organisational context moderators. *Human Resource Management Journal*, in-press.

Garavan, T., McCarthy, A., Lai, Y., Murphy, K., Sheehan, M., & Carbery, R. (2020b). Training and firm performance: A meta analytic review of the mediating effects of human capital and employee effect. Working Paper.

IITD—Irish Institute of Training & Development. (2019). *Enabling the workforce of the future: The role of learning and development*. Available from https://www.iitd.ie/Portals/0/Knowledge%20Centre/webversion_IITD-EnablingTheWorkforceOfTheFuture.pdf?ver=2019-12-03-140907-963.

Kim, Y., & Ployhart, R. E. (2014). The effects of staffing and training on firm productivity and profit growth before, during and after the Great Recession. *Journal of Applied Psychology, 99*(3), 361–389.

Kirkpatrick, D. L. (1987). Evaluation of training. In R. L. Craig (Ed.), *Training and development handbook: A guide to human resource development* (pp. 301–319). New York: McGraw-Hill.

Kraiger, K., Ford, J. K., & Salas, E. (1993). Application of cognitive, skill-based and affective theories of learning outcomes to new methods of training evaluation. *Journal of Applied Psychology, 78,* 311–328.

Messersmith, J. G., Patel, P. C., Lepak, D. P., & Gould-Williams, J. S. (2011). Unlocking the black box: Exploring the link between high-performance work systems and performance. *Journal of Applied Psychology, 96*(6), 1105–1118.

Ployhart, R. E., & Hale, D. (2014). The fascinating psychological micro-foundations of strategy and competitive advantage. *Annual Review of Organizational Psychology and Organizational Behavior, 1,* 145–172.

Ployhart, R. E., Nyberg, A. J., Reilly, G., & Maltarich, M. A. (2014). Human capital is dead; long live human capital resources! *Journal of Management, 40,* 371–398.

Sitzmann, T., Brown, K. G., Casper, W. J., Ely, K., & Zimmerman, R. D. (2008). A review and meta-analysis of the nomological network of trainee reactions. *Journal of Applied Psychology, 93*(2), 280–295.

Tharenou, P., Saks, A. M., & Moore, C. (2007). A review of critique of research on training and organizational-level outcomes. *Human Resource Management Review, 17,* 251–273.

2

Definitions and the Evolution of Learning and Development Research and Practice

Abstract The concepts of learning and development are used in different ways throughout the literature. This chapter considered the nature of learning and development and differentiates it from related concepts such as training, education, human resource development, and workplace learning. The chapter then focused on describing the historical evolution of learning and development as an organisational practice and area of research, highlighting its origins from its initial focus on job-based training, to its evolution in the form of classroom learning, eLearning, blended learning and self-directed learning.

Keywords Learning and development · Training · Education · HRD · Historical evolution of learning and development

2.1 Introduction

It is essential in the context of proposing a new model of L&D effectiveness to first of all provide a brief outline of the development of the function. We first of all define a number of key L&D concepts and emphasise their similarities and differences. We then identify five stages

T. N. Garavan et al.
Learning and Development Effectiveness in Organisations,
https://doi.org/10.1007/978-3-030-48900-7_2

in the evolution of L&D in organisations: (a) early industry origins; (b) the emergence of a focus on individuals; (c) the emergence of the L&D profession; (d) the strategic turn in L&D; and (e) beyond the individual and the classroom.

2.2 Definitions of Key L&D Concepts

There is a lot of debate about whether researchers and practitioners should use the term 'learning' rather than 'training'. The debate is discipline related with researchers from industrial psychology showing a preference for the term 'training' (Whelan and Duvernet 2017) and researchers and practitioners from HRM and L&D showing a preference for the term 'learning' rather than 'training'. The difference in emphasis can be explained as follows. Training as a concept is associated with formal classroom-based training activities (Bell et al. 2017). In contrast, both research and practice in HRM acknowledges that employees and workers acquire KSAs through both formal training activities and informal learning processes. For the purposes of this book, we use the term 'learning' because it covers both formal and informal learning in organisations. Therefore, we distinguish learning from training as follows: learning is defined as a process through which employees acquire KSAs whereas training is one formal approach to develop KSAs (Reynolds 2004).

The term 'learning and development' for the purposes of this monograph, is sufficiently broad to incorporate: (a) formal training activities conducted in classroom settings, on-the-job or online; (b) development and education activities that prepare employees for future career goals and roles; and (c) social, collective and organisational level learning. We therefore conceptualise training as an organisational-level activity within the broader domain of L&D. Furthermore, L&D involves both individual and organisational level processes.

2.2.1 Learning

The concept of learning is understood in different ways, however, Honey and Mumford (1992) observed that 'learning has happened when people can demonstrate that they know something that they did not know before... and when they can do something that they could not do before'. These definitions highlight different dimensions; however, a number of common features emerge.

- Learning involves a longer-term change in KSAs. It enhances the potential of individuals to grow, develop and perform effectively in tasks and job roles.
- Learning is an active process that requires active participation or involvement by the learners.
- Effective learning requires ongoing evaluation of progress and feedback.
- The emotions of learners are a particularly important component of the learning process.

2.2.2 Training

Training is a much narrower concept than learning and is often viewed as a tactical approach to the acquisition of KSAs rather than the more strategic concept of human resource development which we discuss later. Boxall and Purcell (2003: 143) suggested that training is often based on a deficit assumption focusing on a performance gap that needs to be addressed. It can also be based on an improvement assumption whereby a satisfactory level of performance can be enhanced or built upon through training. We highlight a number of important characteristics of training:

- Training is for a shorter term and for a more practical purpose.
- Training focuses on the skills, knowledge and attitudes required to carry out a job to the optimum level of performance.
- Training is an activity applicable to all employees—senior management as well as junior employees.

- Training can take place on-the-job, off-the-job in a classroom setting or online.
- Training is related to a specific current job or role within an organisation.
- Training is a short-term activity that is often understood as vocationally oriented.
- Training was traditionally associated with non-managerial employees; however, managerial employees also require training in organisational processes.
- Training is important for imparting technical and mechanical knowledge.
- Training is designed to achieve experienced worker standard in the shortest time period.
- Training is often a collective process where learners attend a training programme; however, it may be one-to-one.

2.2.3 Development and Education

Both development and education are conceptualised as longer-term learning processes. Development in the context of L&D is viewed as a learning process that occurs in a number of ways, through experience, mentoring, coaching, planned and unplanned work experiences, workshops and outdoor development experiences and is viewed as continuous and long term. Development is self-directed, with the learner taking responsibility for the development process.

Development is a less tangible concept than training but is considered more systematic than education. Development is a process or set of planned activities that will help an individual, over time, to develop to their full potential. Development focuses on enhancing a learner's self-esteem and sense of identity. It involves elements of discovery, reflection and change. It may occur in an organisational setting or it may be a more personal set of activities. When we refer to development in an organisation we are primarily concerned with the growth and advancement of employees. The following are key elements of development as a concept:

- Individuals have ownership of their development.
- Development is a flexible and not always systematic process.
- Unlike training, development focuses on the future rather than the present.
- Development requires an openness and willingness to learn from experience.
- Experience is a central part of the development process.

Education is viewed as a major contributor to the learning process both within and outside organisations. Though training and education are closely related and often occur at the same time, education is a broader concept and is oriented towards the future. It focuses on learning that will help the employee to take on a new role, or to do a different job, at some future date. Education is a broader intellectual process because it involves activities, which can change employees' attitudes and increase their knowledge and understanding. It enables employees to adjust more effectively to their working environment and allow them to cope with change. Educational activities are person-oriented rather than job-oriented, and compared with training, the objectives of education are not easy to define in behavioural terms.

Instruction and teaching are two related and important concepts fundamental to understanding L&D in organisations. Instruction is defined as the delivery of information and activities that facilitate a learner's attainment of learning goals. Instruction is also defined as the conduct of activities that are focused on helping learners learn specific things. The terms 'teaching' and 'instruction' are used interchangeably, however, teaching is defined as those learning experiences in which the instructional message is delivered by a human being, not through the use of media such as videotape, textbooks or computer programmes. Instruction incorporates teaching and other learning experiences in which the instructional message is conveyed by other forms of media. The following are important features of teaching:

- The aim of teaching is to facilitate learning.
- Teaching changes the way in which learners can or will behave in the future.

- Teaching involves implementing strategies that are designed to lead learners towards the attainment of specified goals.
- Teaching is a highly interpersonal and interactive activity involving verbal and non-verbal communication.
- In the ideal situation, teaching is relatively systematic and structured.

2.2.4 Human Resource Development (HRD) and Workplace Learning

Human resource development (HRD) is an academic rather than practitioner-focused concept. Harrison (2009) for example, suggested that while it retains its popularity among academics, it never caught on with practitioners. It is often criticised for its emphasis on people as a 'resource' which L&D practitioners consider to be unfeeling and manipulative. McLean and McLean (2001) defined HRD as:

> any process or activity that either initially or over the long term has the potential to develop adults' work-based knowledge, expertise, productivity and satisfaction, whether for personal or group/team gain or for the benefit of any organisation, community, nation or ultimately the whole of humanity.

HRD is considered to be part of human resource or people management that focuses on facilitating and managing work-related L&D to enhance individual, team and organisational performance. Gibb (2013) highlights that HRD is concerned with three dimensions of individuals:

- Cognitive capabilities, which include the processing and possession of knowledge and information and higher order neurological capabilities.
- Capabilities, which are the practical abilities that employees require to perform work roles and which are natural to an individual or can be developed through practice.
- Desired behaviours which include motivation, attitudes, values, emotional intelligence and social skills.

Workplace learning is an additional concept that fits within the scope of L&D in organisations. We confine the concept of workplace learning to two scenarios: (a) the workplace as a learning environment where the workplace itself is the learning context. It includes on-the-job learning processes that are structured in different ways. This version of workplace learning is akin to training in that it is intentional and planned. Stern and Sommerlad (1999) highlight a version of workplace learning where learning and working are intrinsically linked. Here the learning process is informal and employees develop KSAs through dealing with work challenges, learning from mistakes and observation. It is a systemic process where learning occurs while being engaged in productive work activity.

2.3 The Early Industry Origins of Training in Organisations and Initial Research Efforts

Torraco (2016) pinpoints its emergence to the increased demand for trained workers brought about by technological innovation and economic growth. The TWI Service (a partnership between industry and the US War Manpower Communion) was particularly formative in influencing the emergence of training and development as an important practice. It was particularly influential in that it established a technical training programme and developed the four steps job induction programme. By the end of 1945, the TWI had trained 23,000 employees as trainers and certified 1.75 million production supervisors.

As an academic discipline, it has its roots in applied psychology research (Bell et al. 2017). Much of the early training research focused on the evaluation of specific training efforts such as sales training (Sturdevant 1918) and the investigation of rates of learning (Renshaw 1927). Interest in training research started to grow in the 40s with the predominant focus on predicting training success. During this period, research began to be published on training methods and ways of measuring training success (Kellogg 1946). Much of the academic research on training was in the initial stages, conducted in military settings; however, researchers started to focus on research on industrial training. Researchers began to investigate how best to develop supervisory and operator skills (Canter 1951). A particular feature of the early period of research focused on investigation of the transfer of training. This research typically focused on the effectiveness of classroom-based training; however, Benschoter and Charles (1957) focused on comparing classroom versus technology-based training.

2.4 The Emergence of the Classroom and Structured on-the-Job Training in Organisations

During the post-war period, industry in the USA gradually implemented key lessons learned about training during the war. As a consequence, the era of the classroom and on-the-job training took hold. The development of the Instructional System Model (ISD) was particularly influential in setting a framework for the development of systematic classroom structured on-the-job training. The ISD model emphasised five phases of training design—analysis, design, develop, implement and evaluate (Campbell 1984). This approach was initially applied to classroom training; however, it was also applied to structured on-the-job training (Jacobs et al. 1992). The ISD model led to the emergence of the systematic training model which took hold in the UK, Europe, Australia and New Zealand.

A particularly important intellectual contribution to the field of training focused on human capital theory (Becker 1964). While early proponents of training experienced difficulty in financially justifying investment in training, human capital theory argued that training was an investment rather than a cost. Human capital theory argued that firms should invest in specific training which was directly linked to the productive requirements of the organisation. Its influence on the training industry has remained strong and the profession has experienced major challenges in demonstrating that training generates a return on investment for organisations (Cascio 1989; Brinkerhoff 2006).

Research on training during the 1960s, 1970s and 1980s continued to test interventions rather than develop theory (Kraiger and Ford 2007). These studies focused on identifying which methods were more effective and for the first time, researchers began to investigate the impacts of computer-based training. During the earlier part of the 1970s, researchers began to respond to criticisms that training research was not strong on the use of theory. Latham and Saari (1979, for example, utilised social learning theory to investigate the effectiveness of a behavioural modelling training programme designed to enhance supervisors' interpersonal skills. The 1980s saw an increased interest in the study of training transfer (Baldwin and Ford 1988). This research focused on how best to maximise training transfer and ensure that learning is applied on-the-job.

2.5 E-Learning, Digitisation and a Focus on Context in Understanding the Effectiveness of Learning and Development in Organisations

Significant shifts occurred during the mid to late 1980s and early 1990s in terms of the development of training in organisations. In particular, trainers in organisations started to move away from the classroom and make use of instructional technology. Technology was particularly influential in broadening the range of training delivery methods available to organisations. The introduction of computer-based training in the mid-late 1980s and early 1990s led to a major growth in e-learning. However, in the early 1990s the emergence of the worldwide web prompted a revolution in online learning. The peak of the dot.com boom in the early 2000s led to enormous interest in e-learning and during that period, it became big business resulting in (a) the development of large scale off-the-shelf libraries of generic courses, (b) the development of bespoke multimedia online courses by large multi-nationals and (c) the emergence of learning management systems to manage learners and their learning. Disillusionment with traditional e-learning set in relatively quickly and it was frequently compared unfavourably with traditional classroom-based training. In addition, participation rates on e-learning programmes began to decline. More recent developments in technology have resulted in the emergence of augmented and virtual reality (Paquette 2010), game-based learning, open space technology and massive open online courses (Bogdan et al. 2017).

Within the academic field of training, researchers began to investigate the role of context. This included investigation of the broader training context that shaped the participation of employees in training, their learning and training transfer. Aspects of context investigated included: (a) employee perceptions of the work environment; (b) the role of supervisory and peer support; (c) the determinants of motivation to participate and (d) the rate of pre-training contextual factors that contribute to differences in learning outcomes (Maurer and Tarulli 1994; Noe and Wilk 1993). In addition, researchers also made greater use of theory to investigate the different learning outcomes derived from training.

2.6 The Emergence of Business Partnering Approaches, Blended and Social Learning

In 1997, Dave Ulrich published his influential book Human Resource Champions, in which he delineated for roles for HR in organisations, strategic partner, change agent, administrative expert and employee champion. This thinking had an important impact on the way in which L&D was organised. Of particular importance to L&D was the concept of business partnering. This concept emphasised the contribution of L&D to strategic issues and that it needed to be business-oriented. In 2005, Ulrich and Brockbank revised their original model to include five roles: human capital developer, strategic partner, employee advocate, functional expert and HR leader. The Ulrich Model has had a number of important implications for L&D in organisations. In particular, it has given rise to the increased use of distributed technology and a major decline in the welfare of the 'human face' of L&D. Increasingly, the business partnering model has shifted the focus of L&D to process and operational issues. The notion of blended learning first emerged around 2000; however, it took a few years later for it to catch on in organisations. It became known in organisations as a mixture of technology and face-to-face classroom learning; however, within the L&D profession, it became known as a short e-learning course containing underpinning knowledge which was taken before attending a facilitated workshop or structured classroom training scenario (Güzer and Caner 2014). Proponents of blended learning proposed that it was a cost-effective way for employees to acquire knowledge (Yen and Lee 2011); however, it is often heavily skewed to classroom training with only a small proportion of online learning. Larger firms are making use of interactive scenarios in the classroom, online tutorials and webinars. Learners are also participating in online communities and interactive learning courses. Blended learning has brought the traditional classroom into a more technology-oriented learning context evidenced by advances in live e-learning and 'real time learning'.

The continued emergence and rise of social media and the social web resulted in the emergence of social learning. This involved the use of social media in training and in particular, the potential for learners to interact with one another in online courses (Bingham and Connor 2010). The use of social learning technology provided organisations with (a) the ability to upload user-generated content and the sharing of best practices by peers; (b) opportunities for self-directed learning; (c) a platform for the development of learning communities; (d) mobile learning opportunities. In addition to technology-driven social learning, the emergence of social learning theory (Bandura 1977), experiential learning (McCall 1988) and situated cognition (Brown et al. 1989) resulted in an increased focus on informal social learning in the workplace and the emergence of communities of practice. These trends give recognition to findings that (a) learning is fundamentally a social activity; (b) learning is active; (c) knowledge is integrated within communities and (d) effective learning depends on learner engagement (Marsick and Watkins 1990).

Within the academic discipline of training, scholars took two distinct paths. First, some researchers continued to take a learner-centred approach and researched how different training methods interacted with individual characteristics (e.g. age, gender, ability, etc.) to impact training outcomes. In addition, they focused on how online training impacted trainee engagement and learning outcomes (Sitzmann and Ely 2011). The second path taken by researchers emphasised the benefits for teams and organisations (Aguinis and Kraiger 2009). This research began to engage with how training activities impacted firm performance and productivity (Kim and Ployhart 2014). The increased focus on organisational effectiveness was in many ways prompted by the publication of evaluation models by Kirkpatrick (1987) and Phillips (1991). These models emphasised a linear relationship between training and return on investment outcome and have been particularly influential in shaping organisational practice but less so in the context of academic research.

Recently, both research and practice has increasingly focused on learning that occurs beyond the boundaries of formal classroom training (Dragoni et al. 2014). This research has in particular highlighted that the effectiveness of learning is influenced by the organisational context, characteristics of the individual and structured interventions to enhance learning (Bell et al. 2017). In the context of practice and research, increased emphasis is given to personalised and individualised learning (Pelster et al. 2016). This change has come about through the emergence of self-directed learners and new patterns of work and the drive for autonomy. Chamorro-Premuzic and Swan (2016) highlight that organisations increasingly require employees who have 'learnability' or learning agility, the capacity to keep learning and developing new skills and expertise. Next Generation learners increasingly want freedom, the potential to personalise learning, to collaborate, to be innovative and they have a strong desire for speed (Tapscott 2009). These new approaches and expectations require different responses from L&D, something which we consider in later chapters. Figure 5.1 summarises these key stages.

2.7 Summary

In this section, we provided a brief introduction to L&D as a concept and the historical evolution of L&D in organisations and in terms of research. There are many definitions of what constitutes L&D found in the literature and indeed there is much overlap in how L&D is defined in comparison to training, human resource development and education. L&D has, however, emerged as the term that is now most frequently used in practice to describe a variety of training, development and workforce education efforts. L&D as a set of organisational practices and as a research area has a long lineage. As a set of practices, it can trace its origins to after the Second World War, and in terms of research, the first studies of training appeared over one hundred years ago.

References

Aguinis, H., & Kraiger, K. (2009). Benefits of training and development for individuals and teams, organizations, and society. *Annual Review of Psychology, 60*(1), 451–474.

Baldwin, T. T., & Ford, J. K. (1988). Transfer of training: A review and directions for future research. *Personnel Psychology, 41,* 63–105.

Bandura, A. (1977). Self-efficacy: Toward a unifying theory of behavioural change. *Psychological Review, 84,* 191–215.

Becker, G. S. (1964). *Human capital: A theoretical and empirical analysis with special references to education.* New York: National Bureau of Economic Research.

Bell, B. S., Tannenbaum, S. I., Ford, J. K., Noe, R. A., & Kraiger, K. (2017). 100 years of training and development research: What we know and where we should go. *Journal of Applied Psychology, 102*(3), 305–323.

Benschoter, R. P., & Charles, D. C. (1957). Retention of classroom and television learning. *Journal of Applied Psychology, 41,* 253–256.

Bingham, T., & Conner, M. (2010). *The new social learning: A guide to transforming organizations through social media.* Alexandria, VA: ASTD Press / San Francisco: Berrett-Koehler Inc.

Bogdan, R., Holotescu, C., Andone, D., & Grosseck, G. (2017). *How MOOCs are being used for corporate training*. eLearning & Software for Education, 2.

Boxall, P., & Purcell, J. (2003). *Strategy and human resource management*. London: Palgrave Macmillan.

Brinkerhoff, R. O. (2006). Increasing impact of training investments: An evaluation strategy for building organizational learning capability. *Industrial and Commercial Training, 38*, 302–307.

Brown, J. S., Collins, A., & Duguid, P. (1989). Situated cognition and the culture of learning. *Educational Researcher, 18*(1), 32–41.

Campbell, J. P. (1984). Procedures for developing and evaluating vocational training programs. *Journal of Industrial Teacher Education, 21*(4), 31–42.

Canter, R. R. (1951). A human relations training program. *Journal of Applied Psychology, 35*(1), 38–45.

Cascio, W. F. (1989). Using utility analysis to assess training outcomes. In I. L. Goldstein (Ed.), *Training and development in organizations* (pp. 63–88). San Francisco, CA: Jossey-Bass.

Chamorro-Premuzic, T., & Swan, M. (2016). It's the company's job to help employees learn [blog post]. *Harvard Business Review*. Retrieved from https://hbr.org/2016/07/its-the-companys-job-to-help-employees-learn.

Dragoni, L., Oh, I. S., Tesluk, P. E., Moore, O. A., Van Katwyk, P., & Hazucha, J. (2014). Developing leaders' strategic thinking through global work experience: The moderating role of cultural distance. *Journal of Applied Psychology, 99*(5), 867–882.

Gibb, S. (2013). *Human resource development*. Available from https://www.ebsglobal.net/EBS/media/EBS/PDFs/Human-Resource-DevelopmentCourse-Taster.pdf.

Güzer, B., & Caner, H. (2014). The past, present and future of blended learning: An in-depth analysis of literature. *Procedia—Social and Behavioural Sciences, 116*, 4596–4603.

Harrison, R. (2009). *Learning and development*. London: CIPD.

Honey, P., & Mumford, A. (1992). *Manual of learning styles* (3rd ed.). Maidenhead: P. Honey.

Jacobs, R. L., Jones, M. J., & Neil, S. (1992). A case study in forecasting the financial benefits of unstructured and structured on-the-job training. *Human Resource Development Quarterly, 3*, 133–139.

Kellogg, W. N. (1946). The learning curve for flying an airplane. *Journal of Applied Psychology, 30*, 435–441.

Kim, Y., & Ployhart, R. E. (2014). The effects of staffing and training on firm productivity and profit growth before, during and after the Great Recession. *Journal of Applied Psychology, 99*(3), 361–389.

Kirkpatrick, D. L. (1987). Evaluation of training. In R. L. Craig (Ed.), *Training and development handbook: A guide to human resource development* (pp. 301–319). New York: McGraw-Hill.

Kraiger, K., & Ford, J. K. (2007). The expanding role of workplace training: Themes and trends influencing training research and practice. In L. L. Koppes (Ed.), *Historical perspectives in industrial and organizational psychology* (pp. 281–309). Mahwah, NJ: Lawrence Erlbaum Associates Publishers.

Latham, G. P., & Saari, L. M. (1979). Application of social-learning theory to training supervisors through behavioural modelling. *Journal of Applied Psychology, 64*(3), 239–246.

Marsick, V. J., & Watkins, K. E. (1990). *Informal and incidental learning in the workplace*. London: Routledge.

Maurer, T. J., & Tarulli, B. A. (1994). Investigation of perceived environment, perceived outcome, and person variables in relationship to voluntary development activity by employees. *Journal of Applied Psychology, 79*(1), 3–14.

McCall, D. (1988). *Integrating computers into accounting education.* Deakin University Occasional Paper, 106. Geelong, VIC: Deakin University.

McLean, G. N., & McLean, L. (2001). If we can't define HRD in one country, how can we define it in an international context? *Human Resource Development International, 4*(3), 313–326.

Noe, R. A., & Wilk, S. L. (1993). Investigation of the factors that influence employees' participation in development activities. *Journal of Applied Psychology, 78*(2), 291–302.

Paquette, G. (2010). Ontology-based educational modelling: Making IMS-LD visual. *Technology, Instruction, Cognition & Learning, 7*(3/4), 263–293.

Pelster, B., Haims, J., Stempel, J., & van der Vyver, B. (2016). Learning: Employees take charge. *Global Human Capital Trends Report*. Available from https://www2.deloitte.com/us/en/insights/focus/human-capital-trends/2016/fostering-culture-of-learning-for-employees.html.

Phillips, J. J. (1991). *Handbook of training evaluation and measurement methods.* Houston: Gulf.

Renshaw, S. (1927). An experiment on the learning of "paired associates". *Journal of Applied Psychology, 11*(3), 226–233.

Reynolds, J. (2004). *Helping people learn.* London: CIPD.

Sitzmann, T., & Ely, K. (2011). A meta-analysis of self-regulated learning in work-related training and educational attainment: What we know and where we need to go. *Psychological Bulletin, 137,* 421–442.

Stern, E., & Sommerlad, L. (1999). *Workplace learning, culture and performance*. London: Institute of Personnel and Development.

Sturdevant, C. R. (1918). Training course of the American steel and wire company. *Journal of Applied Psychology, 2,* 140–147.

Tapscott, D. (2009). *Grown up digital: How the net generation is changing your world*. New York: McGraw-Hill.

Torraco, R. J. (2016). Early history of the fields of practice of training and development and organization development. *Advances in Developing Human Resources, 18,* 439–453.

Ulrich, D. (1997). *Human resource champions: The next agenda for adding value and delivering results*. Boston, MA: Harvard Business School Press.

Ulrich, D., & Brockbank, W. (2005). *The HR value proposition*. Boston: Harvard Business School Press.

Whelan, T., & Duvernet, A. (2017). *Learning about learning: Trends in workplace training 2: Trend harder*. Available from https://www.siop.org/ResearchPublications/TIP/TIP-Back-Issues/2017/July/ArtMID/20297/ArticleID/1583/LearningAbout-Learning-Trends-in-Workplace-Training-2-Trend-Harder.

Yen, J. C., & Lee, C. Y. (2011). Exploring problem-solving patterns and their impact on learning achievement in a blended learning environment. *Computers & Education, 56,* 138–145.

3

Theoretical Perspectives and Context of Learning and Development Effectiveness in Organisations

Abstract There are numerous theoretical perspectives that researchers have used to study the effectiveness of training in organisations. We describe and evaluate four theoretical perspectives (universalistic, contingency, configurational and architectural) that researchers have used to explain training effectiveness. We then evaluate a selection of theoretical perspectives including human capital theory, the resource-based view, the behavioural approach, social exchange theory, the behavioural approach, ability-motivation-opportunity theory and attribution theory, each of which suggests different reasons for a link between training and effectiveness. The chapter concludes with a discussion of external and internal contextual factors that shape training effectiveness in organisations.

Keywords Theoretical perspectives · Universalistic perspective · Contingency perspective · Configurational perspective · Architectural perspective · Theories explaining effectiveness · Context of learning and development

T. N. Garavan et al.
Learning and Development Effectiveness in Organisations,
https://doi.org/10.1007/978-3-030-48900-7_3

3.1 Introduction

In this section we describe some of the theoretical perspectives and specific theories that have been used to explain the effectiveness of L&D in organisations. We first of all consider four theoretical perspectives that provide overarching explanations of why and how L&D is effective. These are the universalistic, contingency, configurational and architectural perspectives. We then consider a number of specific theories, some more popular than others, that researchers have used to investigate why and how training impacts organisational effectiveness. The most frequently used theories are human capital theory, the resource-based view, the behavioural approach and social exchange theory. Some of the less frequently used theories are attribution theory and the ability-motivation-opportunity framework. We then consider the changing external and internal context of L&D in organisations.

3.2 Theoretical Perspectives on Learning and Development

3.2.1 The Universalistic Approach to Learning and Development

The universalistic approach to L&D argues that there is one best way to develop employees to achieve organisational performance (Clinton and Guest 2013). This perspective proposes that L&D will have a positive impact on organisational performance irrespective of the size of the organisation, its sector or activities or characteristics of the external environment (Pfeffer 2005). This best practice or universalistic approach is extremely popular with practitioners. It is however, subject to a number of significant criticisms. In particular:

- The perspective does not pay attention to the types and/or quality of L&D in organisations. There is an ongoing debate as to whether firm-specific or general L&D is more effective in achieving organisational performance.

- The impact of L&D in organisational performance may be more impactful where employee skills are essential for organisational performance (Marchington and Grugulis 2000). This suggests that the impact of training will be greater in service organisations and in high-technology organisations.
- The universalistic approach to L&D therefore does not take into account the role of context. For example, Boxall and Purcell (2016) have suggested that a universalistic approach does not take into account an organisation's strategy, its structure, the organisation of work, job roles, employee characteristics and the nature of the external environment.

3.2.2 Contingency Approach to L&D

Whereas the universalistic approach emphasises best L&D practices, the contingency perspective emphasises 'best fit'. It proposes that the L&D practices that organisations use to enhance organisational performance will depend on context. So, for example, these practices will vary by the size of organisation, its life cycle, its strategic direction and industry sector (Kochan and Barocci 1985; Schuler and Jackson 1987). Schuler and Jackson (2014) highlighted a range of contingency or contextual factors that are relevant to explaining why L&D impacts organisational performance. These include: the complexity of the external environment such as market conditions, trade union activities, characteristics of the labour market and factors internal to the organisation including structure, strategy and culture. Fit emerges as a particularly important issue for the contingency perspective on L&D. Two types of fit are highlighted. Vertical fit highlights the fit of L&D with the strategic goals and objectives of the organisation. In contrast, horizontal fit highlights the fit of L&D with other HR practices. In the context of L&D, there is relatively little agreement as to the best mix of L&D practices and which ones best fit together to enhance organisational performance (Noe et al. 2014). How L&D fits with strategy and leads to better vertical fit is therefore unclear. There is little research revealing which L&D practices are a better fit with business strategy. In a similar vein, it is not clear as to how L&D practices fit with other HR practices to maximise organisational performance.

3.2.3 Configurational Approach to L&D

The configurational approach to L&D proposes that organisations have different choices when it comes to L&D practices. For example, Martin-Alcazar et al. (2005) proposed that when organisations select coherent bundles of HR practices including L&D practices, this will lead to enhanced organisational performance. Therefore, where organisations implement several coherent L&D practices, the performance benefits will be greater than is the case for implementing one L&D practice. However, while the configurational approach is attractive in theory, there is much confusion about what should be included in a bundle of L&D practices and how these L&D practices relate to each other. Clinton and Guest (2013) proposed that the effective implementation of a bundle of L&D practices will enhance employee KSAs as well as their motivation to perform. A major unanswered question concerning the configurational approach to L&D concerns the role of context. For example, is there a particular bundle that will work better in say manufacturing versus service industries? Marchington and Grugulis (2000) put forward the notion that the implementation of some L&D practices may undermine the contribution of other L&D practices to organisational performance. Some L&D practices may be more valuable than others; however, we do not know the answer to this fundamental question.

3.2.4 Architectural Approach to L&D

The architectural approach to L&D proposes that organisations should make use of different L&D practices for different groups of employees (McLean and Collins 2011). Therefore, it makes sense for organisations to use different L&D practices depending on the value that particular groups of employees make to organisational performance. For example, core employee groups that are difficult to replace should they leave may receive significant investments in career-focused L&D practices whereas employees who are easier to replace may receive much less L&D investment. There is however not a lot of research highlighting that the architectural approach works in practice. Clinton and Guest (2013) found that there was value in using a full suite of practices for all types of employees; however, this proposition remains relatively untested. The implementation of an architectural approach to L&D is likely very expensive and time consuming. It also requires that L&D professionals are sufficiently skilled to match L&D practices to different employee groups within organisations and it raises problems related to fairness, equality of treatment and perceptions of injustice on the part of employees who receive less investments in L&D.

3.3 Theories Used to Explain the Link Between L&D, Individual and Organisational Performance

So far, we have outlined four broad approaches to explain why L&D is linked to performance. There are numerous theories that can be used to explain how and why L&D is linked to individual and organisational performance. We focus here on six of the more mainstream theories: human capital, the resource-based view, the behavioural approach, ability-motivation-opportunity theory, attribution theory and social exchange theory.

3.3.1 Human Capital Theory

Human capital theory has emerged as one of the most important theories to explain how L&D impacts individual and organisational performance. Schultz (1961) proposed that human capital consists of 'knowledge, skills and abilities of the people employed in an organisation'. In contrast, Bontis et al. (1999: 391) defined human capital as 'the human factor in the organisation; the combined intelligence, skills and expertise that gives the organisation its distinctive character'. Thomas et al. (2013) define human capital as consisting of people, their performance and potential within the organisation. The inclusion of the term 'potential' is instructive because it suggests that organisations can use L&D to develop the skills, abilities and knowledge of employees over time. One of the most important definitions found in human capital theory is the distinction between specific and general human capital. Becker (1964) highlighted that firms would invest in specific human capital because they will gain production advantages from it, whereas investment in general training will not lead to organisational performance advantages. More recent definitions have highlighted an organisation-level focus on human capital. For example, Ployhart et al. (2014) emphasise an emergence perspective whereby individual-level KSAs impact organisation-level outcomes. They make an important distinction between human capital resources and strategic human capital resources. In the case of human capital resources, the outcome is performance parity whereas in the case of strategic human capital resources, the outcome is competitive advantage. So, for example, L&D practices may be used to develop business outcomes such as customer satisfaction, productivity, employee turnover and customer retention. However, formal training is just one contribution that L&D can make. It also includes:

- Workplace learning in the form of learning that is experiential in nature. Eraut et al. (1998), for example, found that non-formal learning plays a major role in developing employee KSAs.
- Self-directed learning which is self-paced and involves employees reviewing what they have learned, identifying learning goals and consideration of how to achieve these goals (Armstrong 2014). Self-directed learning processes are based on the idea that employees will learn and retain more where they find out things for themselves (Smither and London 2009).
- Employee development which involves preparing employees to take on new roles in organisations. Mason and Bishop (2010) highlighted the importance of updating skills to remain competitive and productive. However, employee development is also important for individuals (Armstrong 2014). For example, Fallon and Rice (2015)

found that personal development is a strong predictor for job satisfaction and it will be enhanced through tailored employee development programmes.

3.3.2 The Resource-Based View and Learning & Development

The resource-based perspective view (RBV) is one of the most popular and influential theories to explain how investments in L&D can lead to organisational performance. The basic argument is that investments in L&D result in differences between firms in terms of their potential to achieve competitive advantage. The RBV envisages that firms will in the long term achieve competitive advantage as a result of enhancing the characteristics and value of human resources. The long-term competitive advantage of an organisation will be determined by whether its human resources are valuable, difficult to imitate or substitute, and enable it to differentiate itself from other competitors (Festing and Eidems 2011). Human resources provide the potential for sustained competitive advantage through the use of L&D to develop competencies that are firm specific and to generate organisational tacit knowledge (Lado and Wilson 1994). Tacit and industry-specific knowledge has the most value in a strategic context because this type of human capital is the most difficult for competitors to replicate or copy. The RBV emphasises the need for organisations to implement a specific L&D strategy, one that seeks to achieve competitive advantage by enhancing both the competence and commitment of human resources. It requires that organisations implement an internally consistent set of L&D practices. Research has suggested a set of universal L&D practices that are of value and these include on-the-job training, leadership development, technical competency development, strategies to generate tacit organisational knowledge and social networking (McWilliams et al. 2001).

The RBV can be applied to strategic L&D in a number of ways:

- Development of Core Competencies and Capabilities: It is the competencies and capabilities of employees that are the vital resource for competitive advantage. Hamel and Prahalad (1990), for example, made the argument that where firms had bundles of skills which emerged from the collective learning of employees and work units and they capitalise on these collective skills, they will secure competitive advantage. Core competencies which can be developed through L&D can link learning to the achievement of business strategy. For example, Kamoche (1996) found that employees core competencies were linked to product and service quality.

- Human capital advantage can also confer competitive advantage on organisations. Therefore, L&D can be used to enhance KSAs as well as behaviours and these will lead to competitive advantage. Wright and McMahan (2011) for example, highlighted that highly skilled employees are rare and difficult to source or imitate; therefore, they will bring the most value to the firm.
- Human system advantage can also be a source of competitive advantage. Therefore, L&D can be used to align employees KSAs and motivations with the systems, structures and processes found within an organisation. Wright et al. (2001), for example, proposed that organisations require a mix of human, social and organisational capital to be competitive. Therefore, L&D can be used to integrate these KSAs and motivations into organisation's processes and systems.
- Finally, L&D can provide organisations with competitive advantage through the development of social capital. This dimension emphasises the role of interpersonal and intergroup relationships. Boxall and Purcell (2003) suggested that where L&D facilitates human social capital to operate in a synergistic manner, this can be an important source of competitive advantage for organisations.

3.3.3 The Behavioural Approach

The behavioural approach argues that L&D practices can be used to develop behaviours that will align with an organisation's goals and strategies (Jackson and Schuler 1995). This approach argues that effectively designed L&D policies and practices need to take account of the behaviours that are required to achieve organisational strategies. L&D

can be used to help elicit and sustain from employees the required behaviours. This suggests that L&D will perform a number of important roles:

- It helps to ensure that employees have the competencies required to behave in the ways desired. Competencies are considered an important set of behaviours;
- It helps to motivate employees to demonstrate the desired behaviours on a consistent basis;
- It helps to change the behaviours of employees where they are not aligned with strategies.

There are four important assumptions associated with the behavioural approach. These are as follows:

- The behaviours that employees demonstrate are major determinants of organisational performance;
- The desirability of employee behaviours is influenced by contextual factors such as its size, structure, technology, competitive strategy and industry dynamics;
- L&D can be used to change behaviours because it is assumed that these behaviours are malleable and they can be changed. L&D practices communicate important informational cues concerning how employees should behave;
- An effective set of L&D practices helps to guide employees towards desired behaviours through providing opportunities to engage in these behaviours, developing their competencies to engage in the desired behaviours and through the motivational impact of L&D.

3.3.4 Ability-Motivation-Opportunity Theory

Ability-motivation-opportunity (AMO) theory (Purcell et al. 2003) argues that L&D practices that enhance an employee's ability to perform, motivate them to perform and provide the opportunity to perform will lead to enhanced individual performance. L&D practices can contribute to ability, motivation and opportunity, however, there is some debate as to whether L&D may be more important for some outcomes over others. For example, Bello-Pintado (2015) found that there was a hierarchy within AMO bundles of practices and that motivation-enhancing practices were the most important. An important point of contention concern whether L&D practices are more effective in enhancing ability rather than motivation and opportunity components of the model.

L&D practices are traditionally considered to be ability-enhancing practices. So, for example, extensive formal and on-the-job training will enhance employee KSAs. However, it is also possible to envisage that L&D practices can increase employee motivation where they include a development planning process, employee development activities and career-focused development activities. These motivational effects of training will motivate employees to engage in in-role (task) and voluntary, extra-role (organisational) citizenship behaviours (Guan and Frenkel 2018). L&D practices may also have an opportunity-enhancing dimension where organisations use practices such as empowerment, team-focused L&D and project-based learning.

3.3.5 Attribution Theory and L&D

Attribution theory proposes that L&D practices on their own will not lead to enhanced performance (Nishii et al. 2008). It is the perceptions and attributions that employees make about L&D practices concerning their purposes that is key to understanding their performance impacts. Katou et al. (2014) highlighted content and process dimensions of L&D practices. The content dimension focuses on the types of practices whereas the process dimensions concern perceptions of how effectively they were implemented. Piening et al. (2014) suggested that employees may experience both an interpretation and an implementation gap. The interpretation gap focuses on the differences between implementation and perceptions of implementation, whereas an implementation gap focuses on the differences between the intended and implemented L&D practices. How this plays out in the context of L&D practices is not clear; however, factors that will influence perceptions of implementation will include investment in L&D staff, the skills of L&D professionals and communication processes concerning the implementation of practices. Deficiencies in these components can lead to issues about the intentions of the practices as well as the consistency of their implementation.

3.3.6 Social Exchange Theory

Social exchange theory represents a psychological theory that emphasises the interactions between two parties (Blau 1964). It has emerged as one of the most influential theories in explaining the role of human resource practices in organisations. A social exchange is viewed as a 'two-sided, mutually contingent and mutually rewarding process' (Emerson 1976: 336). Therefore, L&D practices can be understood as creating relationships between employees and the organisation and between employees and their immediate supervisor. The L&D function can be understood as representing the interests of the organisation. In addition, supervisors or line managers are key implementers of L&D in organisations and therefore employees have an interest in engaging in social exchanges with both the L&D function and line managers. Therefore, the implementation of L&D can be viewed as a process that requires exchange between the organisation and the employee and the line manager and the employee, where employees perceive a positive relationship created through the implementation of L&D practices, this can lead to increased individual performance, job satisfaction and organisation performance (Farndale et al. 2011). Therefore, organisations can use L&D practices to enhance social exchange relationships and increase performance for both individual and the organisation.

3.4 The Changing Context of Learning and Development Effectiveness

L&D practices are also impacted by internal dimensions of context. Among the most important context elements are an organisation's strategy, structure, culture, climate and mind-sets.

3.4.1 Organisational Strategy

An organisation's strategy represents one of the most significant internal contextual influences on L&D (Garavan et al. 2019). A key function of L&D is to contribute to the achievement of organisational goals (Wright and McMahan 2011). Strategic alignment is considered vital to the achievement of organisational goals. L&D can contribute to strategic alignment in a number of different ways.

First, L&D contributes to the development of employee capabilities required to achieve organisational strategies. Where employees possess KSAs that are aligned to strategic goals, they can be used to generate value for the organisation (Coff 1997). Second, research highlights the importance of workforce composition to the achievement of strategic goals (Lepak and Snell 1999). Therefore, L&D helps organisations to develop strategic knowledge workers who are strongly strategically aligned with the organisation. Core workers possess skills that are valuable to the organisation. These skills are highly transferable skills and have both high internal and external mobility. Third, the mix of L&D practices that an organisation implements may be important to organisational performance. The appropriate mix of L&D policies and practices enhance an organisation's human capital and impact the creation, transfer and integration of knowledge (Becker and Huselid 1998). We discuss later in this chapter the concept of strategic training and development.

3.4.2 Organisation Structure

An organisation's structure is an important contextual influence on L&D activities and the way in which it is structured. The structure of an organisation is influenced by its mission and strategy. It will typically be designed around its key activities, programmes and strategies. The structure will influence how an organisation manages L&D activities and the extent of centralisation and decentralisation of responsibility for L&D. For example, in the case of multi-national corporations (MNCs) with highly centralised structures will have a strong headquarters that will exert significant control over all foreign operations. MNCs will be structured differently, reflecting key differences in their strategy and goals. Rugman and Hodgetts (2001) suggested, for example, that MNCs will structure themselves in different ways to achieve strategy. They proposed six structural forms:

- International Division Structure: In this situation all international operations are organised into one division. This is typically the structural form adopted by US MNCs and it helps them to develop a cadre of international managers.
- Global Functional Structure: This structure is built around the main functions of an MNC. It is typically found in MNCs that require tight control and operate in materials extraction.
- Global Product Structure: In this structure, parent country divisions are given control over product groups. Each product division is a profit centre and can devote its energies to the needs of a particular product line.
- Global Geographic Area Structure: In this structure responsibility is given to managers for a particular geographic area. It is typically found in MNCs that have narrow product lines and there is a requirement to adapt to local needs and preferences. Managers in this structure require both strong knowledge and an understanding of the MNCs overall strategy.
- Matrix or Three-Dimensional structure: This is a more complex structure and is a mix of product, functional and geographic structures. Employees will report to multiple project managers.
- Network Structure: Typically found in very large transnational MNCs it strives to balance global economies of scale with responsiveness to local customer requirements. It consists of dispersed units or subsidiaries and specialised units.

Domestic organisations tend to be structured in a less complex way in terms of the number of layers and communication channels. These less complex structures will have implications for how work is designed, the tasks that employees perform, the roles of managers and the competencies and skills required to work within the structure (Saks and Haccoun

2013). In small firms, for example, there may be a lot of flexibility and L&D may be more organically organised.

3.4.3 Organisation Cultures, Climate and Mind-Set

An organisation's culture influences L&D because these practices are often used to communicate the organisation culture to employees. The foundations of culture will be found in organisational values and goals. Organisations will use a variety of L&D processes to cascade these values throughout the organisation. In MNCs, for example, the focus may be on developing a homogenous culture with little variation across geographic locations (Punnett and Greenidge 2009). Organisational climate is less frequently highlighted as an important internal influence. It is typically defined as the overall morale or satisfaction of the workforce. Strategies that enhance organisational climate include empowerment, communication and feedback, meaningful work and training and development opportunities. Given the potential for variation due to differences in employee preferences, the concept of organisational climate is complex in the context of international organisations and MNCs. This suggests that organisations should customise L&D practices to enhance organisational climate. Organisations may also have what are called organisations or managerial mind-sets that will influence L&D practices. These mind-sets are particularly important in the context of global and international organisations.

Chakravarthy and Perlmutter (1985) proposed the ERPG Model which consists of four orientations: ethnocentric, polycentric, regiocentric and geocentric. In the context of MNCs and international organisations, ethnocentric mind-sets will be reflected in the belief that one's own identity is superior to others. This mind-set is reflected where nationals from the MNCs or international organisations home country headquarters believe that home country nationals (HCNs) can best realise the goals of the organisation. As a result, headquarters will make the important decisions about L&D strategy, policies and practices. This mind-set may, however, be challenging for an international organisation that requires strong local input and feedback. It may also result in the neglect of the development of local talent that is not HCNs.

Polycentrism as a mind-set emphasises that local preferences and mind-sets should be followed to effectively fit with local conditions. In the context of international non-governmental organisations (INGOs), for example, local responsiveness and flexibility will be best achieved where this mind-set prevails. It best enables the uniqueness and context of the local organisation to come to the fore. In the context of both MNCs and international organisations it may not be conducive to the sharing of learning across operations and national boundaries and can result in significant waste of resources. Global coordination and control become difficult tasks to achieve under this mind-set.

Regiocentrism emphasises the autonomy of multiple countries within the same general region. It would enable common approaches and decision-making processes in major economic regions or in regions where there is extreme poverty or a common set of economic problems.

Geocentrism emphasises a global perspective where the world is a stage for MNC operations. There is an emphasis on the standardisation of operations and processes which may not fit well with INGOs and other international organisations. In the MNC context, this mind-set enables the development of all talent not restricted by ethnicity, country or location.

3.4.4 The Changing Nature of Careers

A number of important changes have emerged in the context of managing human resources in organisations. These include the changing nature of careers, jobs and work design, changes in the nature of employee contracting, the emergence of talent management and increased personal initiative in planning L&D. Significant changes have taken place in terms of careers. One particular concept is the idea of an international career. Individuals increasingly want to have an international career and they are more likely to move between jobs and organisations (Veeran 2009). Organisations no longer promise life-long employment and employees increasingly do not expect job security (Stahl and Bjorkman 2006). Concepts such as the boundary-less career, emphasise the need for employees to accumulate transferable knowledge, a high level of personal investment in one's career, and an emphasis on several potential employees. International managers and expatriates are a major feature of MNCs and international organisations. Expatriates undertake international assignments to enhance their personal and career development opportunities. Ongoing career development is a key feature of successful international careers and employees are expected to take personal control of self-managed or self-initiated expatriates (Haslberger and Vaiman 2013).

Therefore, organisations provide various developmental supports and L&D opportunities for employees at all levels in home and host country locations. A major issue for international assignees and expatriates is their career management on completion of an international assignment. Home country management may not appreciate the career development and experience gained abroad and it may also be under appreciated at head office with the result that the assignee is out of the loop in terms of career opportunities (Van der Heijden et al. 2009). Frequently international assignees and expatriates receive very little career support and they often seek employment elsewhere (McCaughey and Bruning 2005).

3.4.5 Changing Nature of Jobs and Work Design

The landscape of jobs has significantly altered. Technological changes and globalisation have changed the content of jobs, the types of jobs that employees perform and the way in which jobs are designed (Morgeson and Humphrey 2006). The number of knowledge and technology-based jobs has increased (Trent 2007), and the way in which employees perform work is significantly different. Traditional work arrangements are less common and there is major growth in telecommunications, job-sharing, hot-desking and greater flexibility, all of which allow employees to perform work outside of the office. Individual employees increasingly influence the design of their work to allow work to be performed independently at home or at a location convenient to an employee (Cascio 2000; Collings et al. 2010). The design of work to support flexibility is a global phenomenon. In the Netherlands, for example, approximately 18% of workforce is engaged in telework with approximately 137 million employees worldwide engaged in either part of full-time telework. Employees worldwide have a desire for more telework opportunities with the potential to control their work time and to achieve better work–life balance. Organisations have introduced a variety of HR practices such as flexible work arrangements to respond to these expectations. Abendroth and den Dulk (2011) in a survey of 7867 employees in eight European countries, found that when organisations supported work–life balance initiatives, it resulted in greater work satisfaction. Chou and Cheung (2013) found that in Hong Kong, for example, the implementation of family friendly policies was largely voluntary and at the employer's discretion. Chandra (2012) compared Eastern and Western perspectives on work–life balance and found that American MNCs focused on flexible working practices whereas Indian organisations focused on welfare, recreational, health and education initiatives.

3.4.6 The Changing Nature of Employee Contracting

Significant changes have and continue to occur in employee contracting including job crafting (Wrzesniewski and Dutton 2001), idiosyncratic deals (Rousseau 2001), employee voice opportunities (Dyne et al. 2003), personal initiative and taking charge of development. The increased use of individual contracting or unique employment contracts between employees about working conditions is on the increase. The extent to which these work arrangements and other dimensions of the psychological contract are influenced by national cultural differences. Towers Perrin (2008) in a study of 18 countries, asked people to rank the features that attracted them to a firm and the features that would engage employees once employed. Chinese managers, for example, have been slower to adopt 'Western' contract dimensions. Indian employees value input into decision-making and to be kept engaged, and want senior management to adopt actions consistent with values. In the USA, the emphasis is on managers demonstrating an interest in employee well-being and in providing opportunities to enhance skills. Cultural differences have been found to influence other aspects of employment (Chen 2010; Tymon et al. 2010). In countries high on power distance such as Mexico. India, Indonesia and the Middle East, organisations will include terms that emphasise status differences. In high power distance cultures, there will be limited expectation about participation in development activities and decisions will be made by senior management. In contrast, countries with low power distance such as Austria, Ireland, Sweden and Denmark, there will be an emphasis on joint decision-making when it comes to development.

3.4.7 The Emergence of Talent Management

Talent management has emerged as an important organisational practice in terms of managing people that has important implications for L&D. Many organisations and particularly MNCs, have implemented talent management. Traditional perspectives on global talent emphasise a narrow focus on strategically important employees, those who are high performing and they seek to maximise the contribution of a small group of employees (Collings et al. 2018) to organisational performance. Vance et al. (2009) found that many MNCs predominantly focused on the needs of headquarters—home country nationals (HCNs) or parent country nationals (PCNs) expatriates who were working abroad and those returning to the MNCs home country. These groups form only a small percentage of an MNC's employees in a foreign location. Third country nationals are those employed working for a foreign subsidiary who are neither from the host or home country. Singh et al. (2019) suggested that third country nationals are more responsive to local business cultural demands than PCNs. Perspectives on global talent management do not focus on these groups to any great extent thereby neglecting a major group of employees within the global workforce who are strategically important. Vance and Paik (2015) for example, have argued that MNCs cannot separate what they produce or the services they provide from the employees who produce or provide them. They should therefore consider employees that are available to them. Such an approach is more beneficial because it helps to enhance innovation, learning, performance and engagement. The challenge for L&D in this context is to develop all employees and ensure diversity. In addition, there is an increased emphasis on high performance work practices. These practices are typically used to develop employees' abilities, enhance motivation and provide opportunities for development (Combs et al. 2006). High performance work practices include practices such as L&D, intensive training, job autonomy, empowerment and professional development related to future careers. These high performance work practices contribute to both individual and organisational performance.

3.4.8 Personal Initiative and L&D

Personal responsibility for L&D is central to contemporary thinking about L&D in organisations. Personal initiative is defined as a self-starting behaviour. Individuals are expected to be goal directed, long-term focused, action oriented and persistent in pursuit of L&D (Frese et al. 2007). Employees are expected to plan their development by choosing development opportunities, negotiating development assignments and taking responsibility to complete those development activities. King (2004) identified three self-managing behaviours that are relevant to individuals who craft their development. They position themselves and make sure that they have contacts, skills and experiences to achieve development outcomes; they change the amount and/or the quality of social interaction with others who are important for their development and they make strategic choices about development opportunities. McCauley and Hezlett (2002) proposed the notion of self-directed learning as a key for all employees. This involves self-initiated development and sustained pursuit of development opportunities with the goal of enhancing competencies and skills. Employees who are productive when it comes to development exhibit a number of characteristics:

- They have high levels of emotional resilience and therefore can learn from experience.

- They have a strong learning orientation and have the capacity to learn from failure.
- They seek out new challenges, they are organised, positive and show persistence when they experience obstacles.

3.5 Summary

In this chapter we presented a number of high-level theoretical perspectives and specific theories that researchers have used to understand the effectiveness of L&D in organisations. Universalistic perspectives emphasise that L&D will be effective in all types of organisations whereas the contingency perspective highlights the role of context in influencing effectiveness. The configurational perspective highlights the need to combine different L&D approaches whereas the architectural approach emphasises the need to use different L&D strategies depending on the employee group. Human capital and the resource base view emphasise the contribution of L&D to achieving a unique organisational human resource based whereas the behavioural approach highlights the contribution of L&D to developing behaviours that are aligned with business strategy. Social exchange theory emphasises the value of L&D in enhancing the relationship between the organisation and employees whereas attribution theory focuses on the attributions that employees make about the effectiveness of L&D practices. The AMO model highlights the contribution of L&D to enhancing employee ability, motivation and opportunity. Finally, L&D has to respond to a complex array of internal and external factors including changes in the external environment, business strategy, structure and cultural changes, changes in approaches to work and changing expectations of employees.

References

Abendroth, A. K., & den Dulk, L. (2011). Support for work-life balance in Europe: The impact of state, workplace and family support on work-life balance satisfaction. *Work, Employment & Society, 25,* 234–256.

Armstrong, P. (2014). Limits and possibilities for HRM in an age of management accountancy. In J. Storey (Ed.), *New perspectives on human resource management* (pp. 154–166). Abingdon, Oxford: Routledge.

Becker, B. E., & Huselid, M. A. (1998). High performance work systems and firm performance: A synthesis of research and managerial implications. *Research in Personnel and Human Resources Management, 16,* 53–101.

Becker, G. S. (1964). *Human Capital: A theoretical and empirical analysis with special references to education.* New York: National Bureau of Economic Research.

Bello-Pintado, A. (2015). Bundles of HRM practices and performance: Empirical evidence from a Latin American context. *Human Resource Management Journal, 25,* 311–330.

Blau, P. M. (1964). *Exchange and power in social life.* NY: Wiley.

Bontis, N., Dragonetti, N. C., Jacobsen, K., & Roos, G. (1999). The knowledge toolbox: A review of the tools available to measure and manage intangible resources. *European Management Journal, 17,* 391–402.

Boxall, P., & Purcell, J. (2003). *Strategy and human resource management.* London: Palgrave Macmillan.

Boxall, P., & Purcell, J. (2016). *Strategy and human resource management.* London: Palgrave Macmillan.

Cascio, W. F. (2000). Managing a virtual workplace. *Academy of Management Perspectives, 14,* 81–90.

Collings, D. G., Mellahi, K., & Cascio, W. F. (2018). Global Talent management and performance in multinational enterprises a multilevel approach. *Journal of Management.* https://doi.org/10.1177/0149206318757018.

Chakravarthy, B., & Perlmutter, H. (1985). Examining four strategic planning systems available to the MNC in managing the growing complexity of strategic planning. *Columbia Journal of World Business, 20*(3), 3–10.

Chandra, V. (2012). Work / life balance: Eastern and western perspectives. *International Journal of Human Resource Management, 23,* 1040–1056.

Chen, H. F. (2010). The relationships of organizational justice, social exchange, psychological contract and expatriate adjustment: An example of Taiwanese business expatriates. *International Journal of Human Resource Management, 21,* 1090–1107.

Chou, K. L., & Cheung, K. C. K. (2013). Family-friendly policies in the workplace and their effect on work / life conflicts in Hong Kong. *International Journal of Human Resource Management, 24,* 3872–3885.

Clinton, M., & Guest, D. E. (2013). Testing universalistic and contingency HRM assumptions across job levels. *Personnel Review, 42,* 529–551.

Coff, R. (1997). Human assets and management dilemmas: Coping with hazards on the road to resource-based theory. *Academy of Management Review, 22*(2), 374–402.

Collings, D. G., Demirbag, M., Mellahi, K., & Tatoglu, E. (2010). Strategic orientation, human resource management practices and organizational outcomes: Evidence from Turkey. *International Journal of Human Resource Management, 21,* 2589–2613.

Combs, J., Liu, Y., Hall, A., & Ketchen, D. (2006). How much do high-performance work practices matter? A meta-analysis of their effects on organizational performance. *Personnel Psychology, 59,* 501–528.

Dyne, L. V., Ang, S., & Botero, I. C. (2003). Conceptualizing employee silence and employee voice as multidimensional constructs. *Journal of Management Studies, 40,* 1359–1392.

Emerson, R. M. (1976). Social exchange theory. *Annual Review of Sociology, 2,* 335–362.

Eraut, M., Alderton, J., Cole, G., & Senker, P. (1998). *Development of knowledge and skills in employment (Research report 5).* Brighton: University of Sussex, Institute of Education.

Fallon, B., & Rice, S. (2015). Investment in staff development within an emergency services organisation: Comparing future intention of volunteers and paid employees. *International Journal of Human Resource Management, 26,* 485–500.

Farndale, E., Van Ruiten, J., Kelliher, C., & Hope-Hailey, V. (2011). The influence of perceived employee voice on organizational commitment: An exchange perspective. *Human Resource Management, 50,* 113–129.

Festing, M., & Eidems, J. (2011). A process perspective on transnational HRM systems: A dynamic capability-based analysis. *Human Resource Management Review, 21*(3), 162–173.

Frese, M., Garst, H., & Fay, D. (2007). Making things happen: Reciprocal relationships between work characteristics and personal initiative in a four-wave longitudinal structural equation model. *Journal of Applied Psychology, 92,* 1084–1102.

Garavan, T. N., Heneghan, S., O'Brien, F., Gubbins, C., Lai, Y., Carbery, R. et al. (2019). L&D professionals in organisations: Much ambition, unfulfilled promise. *European Journal of Training & Development, 44*(1), 1–86.

Guan, X., & Frenkel, S. (2018). How HR practice, work engagement and job crafting influence employee performance. *Chinese Management Studies, 12,* 591–607.

Hamel, G., & Prahalad, C.K. (1990, May / June). The core competence of the corporation. *Harvard Business Review, 68,* 79–91.

Haslberger, A., & Vaiman, V. (2013). Self-initiated expatriates. In A. Haslberger & V. Vaiman (Eds.), *Talent Management of self-initiated expatriates: A neglected source of global talent* (pp. 1–15). Dordrecht: Springer.

Jackson, S. E., & Schuler, R. S. (1995). Understanding human resource management in the context of organizations and their environments. *Annual Review of Psychology, 46,* 237–264.

Kamoche, K. (1996). Strategic human resource management within a resource-capability view of the firm. *Journal of Management Studies, 33,* 213–233.

Katou, A. A., Budhwar, P. S., & Patel, C. (2014). Content vs. process in the HRM-performance relationship: An empirical examination. *Human Resource Management, 53,* 527–544.

King, Z. (2004). Career self-management: Its nature, causes and consequences. *Journal of Vocational Behaviour, 65,* 112–133.

Kochan, T. A., & Barocci, T. A. (1985). *Human resource management and industrial relations: Text, readings and cases.* Boston, MA: Little, Brown.

Lado, A. A., & Wilson, M. C. (1994). Human resource systems and sustained competitive advantage: A competency-based perspective. *Academy of Management Review, 19*(4), 699–727.

Lepak, D. P., & Snell, S. A. (1999). The human resource architecture: Toward a theory of human capital allocation and development. *Academy of Management Review, 24,* 31–48.

Marchington, M., & Grugulis, I. (2000). 'Best practice' human resource management: Perfect opportunity or dangerous illusion? *International Journal of Human Resource Management, 11,* 1104–1124.

Martin-Alcazar, F., Romero-Fernandez, P. M., & Sánchez-Gardey, G. (2005). Strategic human resource management: Integrating the universalistic, contingent, configurational and contextual perspectives. *International Journal of Human Resource Management, 16,* 633–659.

Mason, G., & Bishop, K. (2010). *Adult training, skills updating and recession in the UK: The implications for competitiveness and social inclusion*, LLAKES Research Paper 19. London: Institute of Education, LLAKES.

McCaughey, D., & Bruning, N. S. (2005). Enhancing opportunities for expatriate job satisfaction: HR strategies for foreign assignment success. *Human Resource Planning, 28,* 21–30.

McCauley, C. D., & Hezlett, S. A. (2002). Individual development in the workplace. In N. Anderson, D. S. Ones, H. K. Sinangil, & C. Viswesvaran (Eds.), *Handbook of industrial work and organizational psychology, vol. 1: Personnel psychology* (pp. 313–335). Thousand Oaks, CA: Sage.

McLean, E., & Collins, C. (2011). High commitment HR practices, employee effort and firm performance: Investigating the effects of HR practices across employer groups within professional firms. *Human Resource Management, 50,* 341–363.

McWilliams, A., Van Fleet, D. D., & Wright, P. M. (2001). Strategic management of human resources for global competitive advantage. *Journal of Business Strategies, 18*(1), 1–24.

Morgeson, F. P., & Humphrey, S. E. (2006). The work design questionnaire (WDQ): Developing and validating a comprehensive measure for assessing job design and the nature of work. *Journal of Applied Psychology, 91,* 1321–1339.

Nishii, L. H., Lepak, D. P., & Schneider, B. (2008). Employee attributions of the 'why' of HR practices: Their effects on employee attitudes and behaviours, and customer satisfaction. *Personnel Psychology, 61*(3), 503–545.

Noe, R. A., Clarke, A. D., & Klein, H. J. (2014). Learning in the 21st century workplace. *Annual Review of Organizational Psychology and Organizational Behaviour, 1,* 245–275.

Pfeffer, J. (2005). Seven practices of successful organizations. In A. Bettley, D. Mayle, & T. Tantoush (Eds.), *Operations management: A strategic approach* (p. 224). London: Sage.

Piening, E. P., Baluch, A. M., & Ridder, H. G. (2014). Mind the intended / implemented gap: Understanding employees' perceptions of HRM. *Human Resource Management, 53,* 545–567.

Ployhart, R. E., Nyberg, A. J., Reilly, G., & Maltarich, M. A. (2014). Human capital is dead; long live human capital resources! *Journal of Management, 40,* 371–398.

Punnett, B. J., & Greenidge, D. (2009). Cultural mythology and global leadership in the Caribbean Islands. In E. H. Kessler & D. K. Wong-MingJi

(Eds.), *Cultural mythology and global leadership* (pp. 65–78). Cheltenham, UK: Edward Elgar.

Purcell, J., Hutchinson, S., Kinnie, N., Rayton, B., & Swart, J. (2003). *Understanding the people and performance link: Unlocking the black box*. London: CIPD.

Rousseau, D. M. (2001). The idiosyncratic deal: Flexibility versus fairness? *Organizational Dynamics, 29*(4), 260–273.

Rugman, A., & Hodgetts, R. (2001). The end of global strategy. *European Management Journal, 19,* 333–343.

Saks, A. M., & Haccoun, R. R. (2013). *Managing performance through training and development* (6th ed.). Toronto: Thomson Nelson.

Schuler, R. S., & Jackson, S. E. (1987). Linking competitive strategies with human resource management practices. *Academy of Management Executive, 1*(3), 207–219.

Schuler, R. S., & Jackson, S. E. (2014). Human resource management and organizational effectiveness: Yesterday and today. *Journal of Organizational Effectiveness: People and Performance, 1,* 35–55.

Schultz, T. W. (1961). Investment in human capital. *American Economic Review, 51*(1), 1–17.

Singh, D., Pattnaik, C., Lee, J. Y., & Gaur, A. S. (2019). Subsidiary staffing, cultural friction, and subsidiary performance: Evidence from Korean subsidiaries in 63 countries. *Human Resource Management, 58*(2), 219–234.

Smither, J. W., & London, M. (2009). Best practices in performance management. In J. W. Smither & M. London (Eds.), *Performance management: Putting research into action* (pp. 585–625). San Francisco, CA: Jossey-Bass.

Stahl, G. K., & Bjorkman, I. (2006). *Handbook of research in international human resource management*. Cheltenham, UK: Edward Elgar.

Thomas, H., Smith, R. R., & Diez, F. (2013). *Human capital and global business strategy*. Cambridge: Cambridge University Press.

Towers Perrin. (2008). *Closing the engagement gap: A road map for driving superior business performance*. Available from https://c.ymcdn.com/sites/simnet.site-ym.com/resource/group/066D79D1-E2A8-4AB5-B621-60E58640FF7B/leadership_workshop_2010/towers_perrin_global_workfor.pdf.

Trent, R. J. (2007). *Strategic supply management: Creating the next source of Competitive advantage*. Plantation, FL: J. Ross Publishing.

Tymon, W. G., Jr., Stumpf, S. A., & Doh, J. P. (2010). Exploring talent management in India: The neglected role of intrinsic rewards. *Journal of World Business, 45,* 109–121.

Van der Heijden, J. A., Van Engen, M. L., & Paauwe, J. (2009). Expatriate career support: Predicting expatriate turnover and performance. *International Journal of Human Resource Management, 20,* 831–845.

Vance, C. M., & Paik, Y. (2015). *Managing a global workforce.* New York: Routledge.

Vance, C. M., Vaiman, V., & Andersen, T. (2009). The vital liaison role of host country nationals in MNC knowledge management. *Human Resource Management, 48,* 649–659.

Veeran, K. (2009). Impact of global economic crisis on HR strategies: Challenges and issues. *Political Economy Journal of India, 18*(2), 1–14.

Wright, P. M., & McMahan, G. C. (2011). Exploring human capital: Putting 'human' back into strategic human resource management. *Human Resource Management Journal, 21,* 93–104.

Wright, P. M., Dunford, B. B., & Snell, S. A. (2001). Human resources and the resource-based view of the firm. *Journal of Management, 27*(6), 701–721.

Wrzesniewski, A., & Dutton, J. E. (2001). Crafting a job: Revisioning employees as active crafters of their work. *Academy of Management Review, 26,* 179–201.

4

A Model of Learning and Development Effectiveness in Organisations

Abstract This chapter presents an open system informed model of training effectiveness in organisations. The model is composed of inputs, process components and outputs. The inputs consist of macro external inputs, internal micro-level inputs and training design inputs. The process elements of the model consist of three components: individual and organisational reactions to training, individual and organisational learning outcomes, and individual and organisational-level training transfer factors. The outputs component of the model consists of emergence enablers, collective human resource outcomes, operational performance outcomes and financial outcomes. The chapter summarises the literature on each component of the model.

Keywords Training inputs · Macro environmental inputs · Micro organisational inputs · Training design inputs · Training reactions · Learning · Training transfer · Emergent enablers · Human resource outcomes · Operational and financial outcomes

T. N. Garavan et al.
Learning and Development Effectiveness in Organisations,
https://doi.org/10.1007/978-3-030-48900-7_4

4.1 Introduction

In this chapter, we present our model (Fig. 4.1) depicting the factors that explain L&D effectiveness in organisations. While the previous chapter provided some high-level analysis in this chapter we go into the specifics of our model. To develop this model, we reviewed the last 30+ years of work on L&D in organisations, including theoretical and empirical contributions. Our aim in developing this model was: (1) to capture the range of micro and macro-level inputs including environmental, organisational and individual that impact L&D in organisations; (2) to understand the individual and organisational processes within organisations that influence reactions to training and its potential value; (3) to map the types of individual and organisational-level learning outcomes that arose in the context of participation in formal L&D; (4) to delineate the factors that influence both individual and organisational-level transfer and (5) the emergent enablers and different organisational-level outcomes that are derived from L&D. We now present each component in detail in the remaining sections of this chapter.

4.2 Learning and Development Inputs

4.2.1 Environmental Inputs to L&D

Globalisation: Globalisation has emerged as one of the key external influences impacting L&D in organisations. It gives emphasis to the reality that many organisations now operate on a global or international scale. Increasingly globalisation impacts the different cultures and contexts in which L&D operates (Sparrow 2007). Scholars highlight three different approaches to understanding the issues that arise for organisations operating in global environments—international, comparative and cross-cultural approaches (McNamara et al. 2011). International approaches emphasise L&D strategies, systems and practices in different socio-cultural contexts and geographies. This approach highlights that a multiplicity of variables will influence L&D issues that

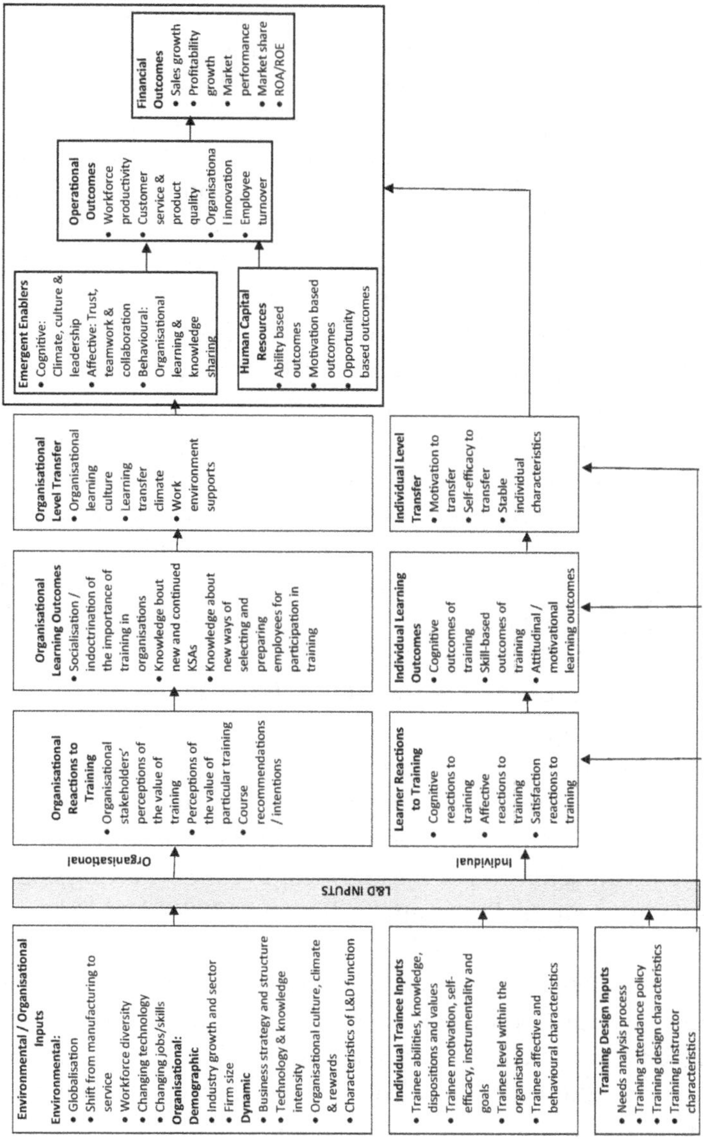

Fig. 4.1 Model Explaining L&D Effectiveness in Organisations

arise in international and global contexts. These include: (a) contextual factors such as country legal systems and cultural distance between the host country and the country of origins; (b) firm-specific factors including the context of internationalisation, industry type and MNC strategy and (c) firm-specific variables such as staff availability, the location of decision-making concerning L&D and the overall approach that the firm takes to implementing L&D strategy (Budhwar and Sparrow 2002; Stone and Deadrick 2015). In contrast, the comparative approach focuses on national patterns of L&D in different countries and unique country context characteristics (Isenhour et al. 2012). So, for example, factors that potentially are relevant include national cultural dimensions such as individualism and collectivism and their impact on L&D practices. Finally, a cross-cultural perspective gives primacy to the extent to which the values of individual learner's influence both the acceptance and effectiveness of L&D practices (Aycan et al. 2000). It primarily argues for the importance of employees' cultural values and the need for the alignment of L&D practices with these values. For example, in the case of employees who value collectivism, they will have a preference for group-focused learning activities. Stone-Romero et al. (2003) for example, argued that employees in collectivist cultures will be more receptive to feedback than is the case for individualist cultures.

Shifts from a Manufacturing to a Knowledge Economy: The shift from a manufacturing to a knowledge economy is highlighted as one of the most significant external factors influencing L&D in organisations. The research points to the emergence of the knowledge economy that emphasises the use of knowledge and information to create business value. The characteristics of the knowledge economy are highlighted by various commentators. For example, Tapscott (2009) highlights three characteristics: knowledge as the key production factor; the knowledge economy is a digital economy and virtualisation plays a key role in the operation of the knowledge economy. In contrast, White et al. (2012) suggest four micro characteristics of the knowledge economy: open innovation, education, knowledge management and creativity.

The emergence of the knowledge economy places very significant demands on organisations' L&D practices. For example, many of the assumptions that underpin traditional approaches to L&D may not have relevance to the knowledge economy. In the case of knowledge organisations, a particular primacy is placed on employees' KSAs because they are considered vital to organisational success (Ricceri 2008). In addition, knowledge organisations emphasise job designs that encourage continuous learning, innovation, empowerment and continuous improvement. These new job requirements require that L&D refocus its provision to develop unique skill sets and abilities. L&D is more likely to be used as an important practice to retain highly skilled employees and meeting the varied and multiple skill needs of knowledge workers. Given the primacy of high-quality KSAs to knowledge organisations, it therefore represents an important opportunity to raise the strategic profile and contribution of L&D in organisations and make it more critical and central to how the organisations functions.

Workforce Diversity: Diversity in the workplace has emerged as a major external factor that requires organisations to develop L&D practices that align with the values and priorities of multiple generations (Twenge et al. 2010). Various dimensions of workforce diversity are highlighted. First, challenges arise concerning age and generational diversity. Due to major skill shortages organisations are increasingly required to tap into the skills of all generations. These include retention of baby boomers until qualified replacements are found (Cheung and Wu 2013) and the provision of L&D opportunities for older employees. In addition, L&D will play a major role in retaining employees of all generations. Newer generations, for example, are more likely to place value on L&D opportunities and the acquisition of skills to enhance employability (Cennamo and Gardner 2008).

An additional diversity issue arises due to ethnicity. Ethnicity diversity is both an opportunity and challenge worldwide and those groups differ in their cultural values and preferences for particular L&D practices (Guerrero and Posthuma 2014). Many L&D practices are frequently designed for a more homogenous workforce in terms of cultural values; however, different ethnic groups have distinctive L&D preferences and development needs (Stone and Deadrick 2015). These ethnic differences require that organisations modify or change their approaches to L&D provision and utilise more customised and individualised approaches (Garavan et al. 2019).

Changing Technology: Major changes have taken place in the increased use of information technology. Technology such as the World Wide Web has transformed how L&D is undertaken in organisations and fundamentally altered the relationship between individuals and organisations (Salas et al. 2005). Scholars increasingly refer to the fourth industrial revolution (Schwab 2016) and its potential to blend hardware, software and people to undertake work in organisations. The emergence of artificial intelligence has emerged as a major technological development (Jarrahi 2018). Artificial intelligence emphasises the extension of cognitive utility involving the use of technology to augment human work. Examples include Chabot and the use of learning management systems to enable the personalisation of learning (Collings et al. 2019).

Another dimension of technology involves the increased use of robots. They are increasingly deployed in organisations across areas such as logistics, production and warehousing (West 2018). Other dimensions of technology highlighted include distributed access and 'self-service' use of mobile device applications, social media applications, use of cloud-based services, sentiment analysis and gamification. According to the KPMG Global HR Transformation Report (2016) many organisations are utilising cloud computing to revolutionise L&D with data-based decision-making. Proponents of the use of technology such as robotics highlight its potential to lead to productivity gains, job creation and greater organisational flexibility. However, it also has major implications for skills development. Technology can help the L&D function to make better decisions about L&D based on objective information and decision support systems (Dulebohn and Johnson 2013). For example, the application of e-learning has enabled L&D to be much more volume focused. Scott-Jackson et al. (2016), for example, found that new technology, specifically mobile technologies, has the potential to alter the way in which people learn.

Changing Jobs and Skills: There is increased evidence that the landscape of jobs and skills are fundamentally altered and will continue to do so. A report by the McKinsey Global Institute (2017), for example, highlights that by 2030 there will be a greater requirement for technical skills, social and emotional skills and a continued use for higher cognition skills. Boudreau (2016) identifies five forces that are shaping the world of work, jobs and skills: (a) social and organisational reconfiguration, to be more flexible, emphasising project-based relationships; (b) an all-inclusive global talent market; (c) a truly connected world where work is increasingly virtual and occurs anywhere and anytime, utilising mobile personal devices with global real-time communication; (d) increased human-automation collaboration through the use of analytics, algorithms, big data and artificial intelligence and (e) exponential technological change. The gig economy has emerged as a major topic of debate (Gallup 2018). This concept involves a 'way of working that is based on people having temporary jobs or doing separate pieces of work, each paid separately rather than working for an employer' (Cambridge Dictionary 2019). These various work changes have important implications for the role of L&D in organisations.

4.2.2 Organisational Inputs to L&D

Business Strategy and Standards: One of the most significant internal inputs to L&D is the organisation's business or corporate strategy. Organisational strategy is concerned with the patterns of behaviour used by the organisation to respond to the external environment (Miles et al. 1978). These strategies have important implications for both the role of the L&D profession and the types of practices that are implemented. Research highlights that organisations with more formal business strategies are more likely to have more aligned L&D practices (Blom et al. 2018). Additionally, the type of strategy utilised by the organisation will have implications for L&D practices. For example, where organisations pursue cost-leadership strategies they are likely to focus on narrow training activities to enhance skills and do so at the lowest cost. In contrast, organisations that pursue a differentiation strategy are more likely to focus on L&D activities that enhance both job specific and broader skills to enable differentiation and achieve competitive advantage (Snow and Hrebiniak 1980).

The impact of organisation structure on L&D practices will be particularly immediate and direct. The dimension of organisation structure that is most relevant concerns whether it is a domestic or international structure. In domestic organisations the L&D approach and activities will be considerably simpler and will be typically organised as part of the HR function (Nadiv et al. 2017). In international organisations L&D practices will be influenced by a strong set of HQ-subsidiary relationships (Farndale et al. 2010). In these types of structures, the extent of L&D practices will be more expansive with a requirement to respond to a more diverse set of needs and L&D requirements. In some subsidiaries with greater distance between the parent and host country there is likely to be more flexibility in terms of the practices utilised.

Organisation Culture, Climate and Reward: Organisation culture and in particular a variant of culture-training culture is emphasised in the literature (Beier and Kanfer 2010). Sitzmann and Weinhardt (2015) conceptualise a training culture as one where the organisation is perceived to support and encourage continuous learning. Dimensions of training culture highlighted include the opportunity to utilise skills developed through training, the availability of resources for training and the frequency of feedback available concerning the effectiveness of skill implementation (Tracey et al. 1995). Other researchers have highlighted dimensions such as employee perceptions of policies supporting training, the prioritisation of training and the extent to which training transfer is encouraged (Maurer and Tarulli 1994). Noe (1986), for example, highlights the role of supervisor and peer attitudes towards training as a key dimension of training culture.

The impact of climate is also highlighted as an important micro-level input that determines training effectiveness. Organisational climate is conceptualised as 'the current perception of people within a work environment with regard to the observable (social, political and physical) nature of the personal relationships that affect the accomplishment of work within a particular organisation' (Denison 1996: 624). It is argued that a supportive organisational culture facilitates learning, enhances motivation to learn and there is a desire to implement and maintain skill levels (Chadwick and Raver 2015). Quratulain et al. (2019) highlight three dimensions of organisational climate that are central to learning: perceived flexibility, performance feedback and support from supervisors.

Another important micro organisational input concerns the nature of rewards and sanctions that operate in respect of training. Sitzmann and

Weinhardt (2015) argue that the persistence of employees to achieve training goals will be influenced by the types of rewards or sanctions that are implemented. Where employees perceive that the completion of training is associated with rewards, this is likely to enhance employees training participation and engagement (Hurtz and Williams 2009). On the other hand, sanctions associated with training may also come into play. These sanctions can take the form of disqualifying employees from key positions or disciplinary sanctions, where they fail to participate in training.

Technology and Knowledge Intensity of the Organisation/ Workforce Characteristics: Organisations differ in their technological and knowledge intensity. Where organisations operate in a high-technology context, they will utilise more sophisticated and complex work methods and practices and will make a significant investment in training (Rauch and Hatak 2016). Organisations with a high level of technology and knowledge intensity will derive their competitive advantage from the skills and abilities to create and manage knowledge (Bettis and Hitt 1995). In these organisations, training practices will play a major role in ensuring that employees can acquire as quickly as possible, the critical KSAs for job performance. In contrast, where organisations are characterised by low-technology and low-knowledge intensity L&D practices will be much narrower and job tasks will be simpler.

At a more general level, work and job characteristics will also act as an important influence in training practices. Jobs typically differ in terms of demands and controls (Karasek and Theorell 1990). Job demands emphasise the physical and mental inputs required to complete the work, whereas job control refers to the amount of control that an employee has over work processes. These include the ability to make decisions and the opportunity to exercise a degree of control over the work (Raemdonck et al. 2014). Passive jobs are characterised by low job demands with limited job control, thus resulting in fewer opportunities to learn and develop. In contrast, active jobs provide learners with multiple opportunities to learn and develop. These job characteristics have important implications for both the extensiveness and intensity of training and development.

Industry Growth and Sector Characteristics: The level of industry growth and dynamism that the firm encounters are an important determinant of L&D practices. Where, for example, the firm operates in a low growth context, the primacy of L&D will be significantly lower and there will be less training activity (Kim and Ployhart 2014). In contrast, where the firm operates within a high-growth context, the importance of L&D will be significantly greater with a greater need for continuous learning. In addition, where firms operate in highly dynamic environments there will be a stronger focus on training and development practices. This will be evident in a greater need for more complex and varied competencies. Martinez-Sanchez et al. (2007), for example, found that where there is a need for broad competencies L&D practices will be more strategic, continuous and change oriented.

The sector in which a firm operates will also have an influence on training practices. For example, in service organisations, there will be a greater reliance on broad employee competencies to achieve organisational performance. In manufacturing firms, there will be a major focus on production type training activities where employees have less discretion to use their skills and competencies (Quinn et al. 1997; Rosenthal et al. 1997).

Organisation Size: We conceptualise organisation size as an important demographic organisational characteristic. Research highlights important differences between small, medium and large firms when it comes to training. Rauch and Hatak (2016) for example, found differences between small and medium sized firms when it comes to training. Similarly, Tzabbar et al. (2017) found that the impact of training on firm performance was greater in medium rather than large firms. In contrast, Garavan et al. (2020) found no differences between small and large firms. Theoretically, it is suggested that training will be more effective in large organisations because they have more resources and expertise to design and implement training effectively (Garavan et al. 2016). In addition, smaller firms are more likely to have greater strategic ambiguity and are less likely to adopt a strategic approach to training (Blom et al. 2018; Noe 2017). Large firms are more likely to have less strategic ambiguity and ensure better alignment of training with business strategy.

Characteristics of the L&D Function: Researchers highlight that characteristics of the L&D function are important in influencing L&D practices. Of particular significance are the maturity of the L&D function, the use of technology and characteristics of the L&D role holder. The maturity of the L&D function has implications for the extensiveness and quality of L&D practices (Loon 2016). For example, where the L&D function is at the early stages of development, it will function in more job-based training activities (Gubbins and Garavan 2009). In contrast, where the function is more mature, the focus will be on a broader suite of training practices and a greater focus on the quality of training programmes. An important dimension of maturity concerns the role of technology. L&D functions with greater technological capabilities will utilise different approaches to achieve training goals. Characteristics of the L&D role holder will also be important. These include their management position within the organisation structure, their credibility and expertise and stakeholder perceptions of their ability to contribute to the organisation (Garavan et al. 2019).

4.3 Individual Inputs to Learning and Development

The second set of inputs that we focus on are characteristics of those who will be trained. We focus on four trainee characteristics: (a) trainee level of knowledge and ability; (b) trainee motivation for training and self-efficacy; (c) trainee affective status and (d) trainee level within the organisation.

4.3.1 Trainee Level of Knowledge and Cognitive Ability, Dispositions and Values

Numerous research studies highlight the important role that individual trainee characteristics including cognitive ability, existing knowledge, personality differences and differences in values will influence the level of learning derived from participation in training. For example, cognitive ability is a particularly important training input because of its impact on the types of training goals that are set (Phillips and Gully 1997). It is conceptualised as an individual's capability and is considered one of the strongest predictors of training effectiveness. Therefore, trainee participants with higher levels of cognitive ability will likely learn more and are likely to be better able to perform skills acquired during training (Kanfer and Ackerman 1989).

In terms of dispositional factors, research highlights the important role of conscientiousness, which is defined as a personality trait associated with discipline, organisation dependability, hard work and achievement orientation (Barrick and Mount 1991). Research highlights that trainees high on conscientiousness will achieve higher training outcomes (Barrick et al. 2002). Trainees with high levels of conscientiousness will more likely be motivated to acquire new information, develop plans to reach training goals and show perseverance when they encounter difficulties in implementing training (Sitzmann and Johnson 2012; Colquitt et al. 2000). A trainee's existing level of knowledge is also highlighted as an important input to training. Existing levels of knowledge will impact the level of training achieved. Research has also highlighted the significance of the language level of trainees as an important barrier that will hamper learning and training effectiveness (D'Souza et al. 2012; Menzel and Gutierrez de Blume 2010). Similarly, individual trainee values are also important. For example, Wang et al. (2007) highlighted that an individual's cultural values influence learning.

4.3.2 Trainee Motivation and Self-efficacy, Instrumentality and Goals

Scholars have highlighted the role of both motivations to learn and self-efficacy as important trainee inputs. Motivation to learn refers to the intention of a trainee to invest high levels of consistent effort in a training programme. Research highlights that motivation to learn is important for training effectiveness (Mathieu and Martineau 1997; Tziner et al. 2007). Motivation is conceptualised as an important resource available to learners which is particularly important when the requirement to undertake training conflicts with more immediate work priorities (Baldwin-Evans 2007).

Self-efficacy to learn is defined as a learner or trainee's belief that he/she can meet the requirements set by the training and master the training content (Gist et al. 1991). Self-efficacy to learn emerges as a very important predictor of training effectiveness (Mathieu et al. 1993) and has a particular link with the amount of effort that a trainee will exert to achieve effective training performance. Self-efficacy is particularly important in explaining how trainees prioritise training and the persistence they show to achieve training goals. It follows that where trainees are confident that they will succeed in training, they are more likely to give priority to it over other organisational goals and show confidence in pursuing training goals (Cervone and Peake 1986).

A particularly proximate motivation characteristic concerns instrumentality of training. This concept refers to a trainee's perception that completion of the training will lead to valued and important outcomes. Campbell (1988) highlights that the magnitude of training instrumentality will impact training effectiveness. Training instrumentality emphasises individuals' perceptions that their efforts in training will enable them to gain rewards at work (Guerrero and Sire 2001: 990). In the context of training, there is an expectation that trainees will accrue both intrinsic and extrinsic rewards. The former include personal satisfaction derived from the training whereas the latter emphasise job roles and promotion changes. Tharenou (2001) found, for example, that training instrumentality had a positive impact on training effectiveness. In a similar vein, research highlights the importance of both mastery and completion goals. Completion goals are understood as the desire to complete a training programme in the least amount of time possible and with minimal effort to achieve completion (Cerasoli et al. 2018). An important consequence of a completion goal is the likelihood that a trainee will approach training in a passive way or with potential resentment or resilience (Vancouver et al. 2014). In contrast, mastery goals are of greater value in the context of training. They will be reflected in behaviour to acquire knowledge and skills through participation in training. Strong mastery goals will be reflected in a concern to understand the training context and enjoy the challenges involved in the training.

4.3.3 Trainee Level Within Organisation

Scholars have drawn attention to the level of the trainee within the organisation as an important individual-level input impacting training effectiveness. The available findings suggest that lower level employees may be more motivated to attend because they view it as an opportunity to increase their skills and career opportunities (Richard et al. 2009). In the context of leadership training, for example, research highlights that lower level leaders that lack the necessary skills, will participate in training because of the opportunities for improvement (Lacerenza et al. 2017). There is evidence suggesting that middle and more senior-level employees may perceive that they do not require further development because they have managed to progress effectively based on their current skill level (Quinn et al. 1997).

4.3.4 Trainee Affective States and Behavioural Characteristics

Research highlights a variety of affective and behavioural characteristics that are relevant to training effectiveness. For example, research highlights the important role of trainee job satisfaction and organisational commitment. Job satisfaction refers to an employee's overall experience of their job (Cranny et al. 1992). A positive correlation between job satisfaction and receiving training has been highlighted in various studies (Gu and Chi Sen Siu 2009), for senior managers (Schmidt 2010) and lower level managers (Sahinidis and Bouris 2008). The role of organisational commitment is also highlighted as an important trainee characteristic. For example, where employees have higher levels of organisational commitment, they are more likely to participate in training and to pursue the goals specified for the training.

Scholars have highlighted the important roles of both learning goal orientation and performance goal orientation. According to Seijts et al. (2004) where trainees have a high level of learning goal orientation, they will seek challenging tasks that enable the opportunity to acquire new skills and competencies. They will also be more likely to devote more attention to the training. In the case of performance goal orientation there will be a strong desire to demonstrate competence and impress others. In terms of research the findings indicate that learning goal orientation is associated with higher levels of training success than is the case for performance goal orientation (Vandewalle et al. 2001).

4.4 Training Design Inputs

The third set of inputs central to our training effectiveness model concerns important training design characteristics. We focus on four learning design features that are given particular prominence in the literature: the needs analysis process; the organisation's training attendance policy; training design features and trainer instructor characteristics.

4.4.1 Organisation Training Needs Analysis Process

Research highlights the importance of needs analysis as central to aligning the training content with individual needs (Arthur et al. 2003). Where organisations conduct needs analysis it enables them to better design the training content to address the training gaps identified. However, organisations frequently neglect the needs analysis process because they perceive it to be a waste of time (Garavan et al. 2019). Research also highlights the problems that arise where needs analyses are not undertaken. For example, trainees may perceive that the content of the training programme does not reflect their needs and therefore they may be both less motivated to attend and learn (Collins and Holton 2004).

4.4.2 Training Attendance Policy

The literature reveals that there are potential differences in motivation to attend training and learn depending on whether attendance is voluntary or mandatory (Curado et al. 2015). There are, however, some debates as to which is more effective from a motivational perspective. Some researchers argue that mandatory training will be more effective because it sends a clear message that the organisation is committed to the training, thus increasing the motivation of trainees to learn (Paluck 2006). Colquitt et al. (2000), for example, stresses the importance of positioning training effectively within the organisation. However, the alternative perspective is that giving trainees a choice and the autonomy to attend will, in fact, foster motivation, thus increasing motivation to attend and learn (Cohen 1990). For example, Blume et al. (2010) found a positive correlation between learning transfer and voluntary attendance.

4.4.3 Training Design Characteristics

Researchers point to a number of training design, delivery and implementation characteristics that influence training effectiveness. Training design characteristics highlighted include whether the programme is inclusive or population specific (Bezrukova et al. 2016), training duration (Chen and Jermias 2016), types of learning objectives (Birou et al. 2019), the methods of training used (Dachner et al. 2019) and the sequencing of the training (Baldwin and Ford 1988). An important design consideration concerns the focus of the training—organisation specific versus educational. Therefore, we would expect that trainees may perceive more value in organisation focused rather than broader educational-focused programmes. A second design feature is concerned with whether the training is integrated or stand alone. Where the programme designed is part of a more integrated suite of training programmes, with support from senior members of the organisation, then it may reinforce learning outcomes (Salas and Cannon-Bowers 2001). Third, research highlights that the duration of the training is important. It is argued that where training is of longer duration, then it gives trainees more time together and build confidence to implement the training. In addition, cognitive load theory (Paas et al. 2004) argues that learners have finite working memory, therefore, where there is information overload, this will inhibit learning outcomes. Therefore, where programmes are designed to address cognitive load, then they will be more effective. So, for example, spaced training is generally found to be more effective than massed training (Lee and Genovese 1988).

A fourth training design concerns the types of learning objectives that are set for the training. For example, awareness-based learning objectives focus on enhancing employees' knowledge, values and beliefs (Gusdorf 2009). Skill building learning objectives focus on building the skills of participants. Associated with the type of learning objective concerns the delivery method. Lacerenza et al. (2017) distinguish three categories of delivery methods: (a) methods focused on the delivery of information; (b) methods focused on demonstrating skills and abilities and (c) methods focused on skill practice opportunities. Trainers typically utilise lectures, presentations to disseminate information whereas demonstration-based methods provide employees with negative and positive behaviour examples. Practice-based methods include role-play, simulations, case scenarios and in-tray exercises. Research highlights that the use of practice-based methods are particularly important in influencing training outcomes. An added complication in the context of training method concerns whether they are face-to-face or virtual. Virtual training methods involve training delivered utilising technology. Research suggests that virtual-based training may be less effective than face-to-face training. For example, Magerko et al. (2005) proposed that face-to-face training helps trainers to monitor learner progress and adjust the training where necessary. In contrast, virtually designed training delivery is less interactive thus diminishing training effectiveness. A final dimension of training design concerns the location of the training. In the case of on-site formal training trainees are immersed in the training environment and thus have a context or environment that is highly aligned with the actual work situation. Off-site training programmes will not be able to avail of this advantage (Salas et al. 2015). Where training is conducted on-the-job, there is a higher potential for training effectiveness because it allows for the immediate application of the training. Thus, training context meets the requirements for three types of fidelity: equipment, environment and psychological (Rehmann et al. 1995).

4.4.4 Trainer Instructor Characteristics

Research highlights that the background of the trainer is an important factor in explaining training effectiveness (Kalinoski et al. 2013). Characteristics of trainers highlighted in the literature include their expertise, credibility and whether they are internal or external. In the context of the use of external trainers, research suggests that trainees may perceive them as having greater credibility and expertise (Teckchandani and Schultz 2014). However, research also reveals that internal trainers may be perceived as equally effective especially where they have extensive job knowledge (McCormick 2000). Where trainers possess a deep expertise in the area of training, they are more likely to exert greater effort because they believe the training is important to the organisation.

4.5 Individual and Organisational Related Reactions to Training

Given the nature of the training process and consistent with thinking by Howardson and Behrend (2016), reactions are an essential component of our model. They represent the first set of outcomes that are derived from participation in training. Reactions are conceptualised as the feelings of trainees and other organisational members about the training undertaken (Alliger et al. 1997). These reactions are important predictors of a variety of learning outcomes (Kirkpatrick 1987; Sitzmann et al. 2008). Our model of training effectiveness differentiates individual and organisational-level reactions to training. Individual-level reactions focus on three sub-dimensions: (a) perceived utility of the training; (b) perceived relevance of the training and (c) effective reactions to the training. Organisational-level reactions focus on: (a) organisational perceptions of the perceived quality of the training; (b) perceptions of the utility or value of the training to the organisation; (c) the appropriateness of the training to address the identified needs and (d) the overall reputation of the training programme within the organisation.

4.5.1 Learner Reactions to Training

Reaction evaluation is one of the most ubiquitous training evaluation practices in organisations (Garavan et al. 2019). The debate about the usefulness of reactions as a measure of training effectiveness is not settled, with a lack of a 'strong evidence indicating importance in moving in from reactions to learning to job behaviour and results' (Brown 2005; Blanchard and Thacker 2007). The empirical evidence, for example, reveals a mixed set of findings. For example, Russ-Elf and Preskill (2005) revealed that negative reactions lead to lower levels of learning whereas Tan et al. (2003) found that negative reactions resulted in higher levels of learning. Sitzmann et al. (2008) in a major meta-analysis found that reactions to training predicted pre- to post- changes in motivation and self-efficacy and played an important role in how trainees perceived characteristics of a training programme. However, scholars have highlighted the importance of conducting evaluations of reactions to training. Giangreco et al. (2010), for example, argued that reaction evaluation helped trainers to make decisions about the validity of the training materials, that the programme was effectively planned and administered and that the content was effectively aligned with the needs of participants.

There is a debate as to what constitutes reactions. For example, Howardson and Behrend (2016) emphasised that reactions are not a singular construct but are comprised of multiple dimensions. Warr and Bunce (1995) distinguished utility, difficulty and affective interactions. Alliger et al. (1997) conceptually distinguished utility and affective reactions to training whereas Brown (2005) argued reactions to training have distinct cognitive and affective components and the link between them is liked to overall satisfaction with the training.

Cognitive Reactions to Training: These reaction elements emphasise how trainees think about the training and will typically focus on issues of how they were selected for the training, its timing and value to their career and job. One particular cognitive dimension concerns the utility of the training (Noe 1986). Trainees will assess utility in different ways including: the value of the training for present work responsibilities; the relevance of the content to current learning needs; the value of the content for future development; the extent to which the content was in line with programme objectives (Sebastiano and Bellet 2005) and the balance of the theoretical and practical aspects of the training (Morgan and Casper 2000).

Affective Reactions to Training: Affective reactions are conceptualised as a trainee's feelings about the training undertaken. These affective dimensions will include emotional reactions to the training, frustration or enjoyment with the training and whether the training was stressful or not. Howardson and Behrend (2016) highlight the importance of affective reactions, however, Sitzmann et al. (2008) found that affective reactions were positively, but weakly, related to learning. In particular, the correlations between affective reactions and declarative, procedural and delayed procedural knowledge were not different from zero. Howardson and Behrend (2016) made a distinction between pleasant and unpleasant affective reactions. Pleasant affective reactions include excitement, elation, happiness and alertness. Unpleasant reactions include stress, fatigue, nervousness and sadness. They found that the reactions that are important for reputation of the programme may not be beneficial for learning.

Satisfaction Reactions to Training: Satisfaction reactions can be both cognitive or affective in nature and constitute general evaluations of the training programme. Giangreco et al. (2010), for example, found a strong positive link between perceptions of the utility of a training programme and overall satisfaction. Research suggests that the level of trainee satisfaction with the performance of the trainer had an important impact on the overall satisfaction with the training (Russ-Elf and Preskill 2005). Dimensions of trainer performance that are important include: (a) mastery of the topic; (b) effective delivery of the subject matter; (c) use of time during the training; (d) use of different learning methods and (e) skills to involve the audience.

4.5.2 Organisation-Level Reactions to the Training

Researchers have, to a significant degree, ignored organisation-level reactions to the training. These reactions are important because they will influence future delivery of the training, the amount of resources allocated to training and the overall reputation of training within the organisation. Therefore, while the majority of training research has focused on trainee reactions to training, the reactions of important organisational actors including first-line supervisors, senior managers and executives, as well as L&D practitioners are also important to understand training effectiveness. Given that the implementation of training is facilitated and implemented by multiple actors, their reactions need to be considered in a model of training effectiveness. We focus here on four dimensions of organisation-level reactions.

Organisational Stakeholders Perceptions of the Value of Training in Organisations: It is inevitable that organisational stakeholders will have visibility or exposure to particular training programmes. Therefore, based on those exposures they will have reactions in terms of whether the training meets the strategic needs of the organisation, whether the programme was value for money as an investment and whether future investments in training are warranted (Aguinis and Kraiger 2009). These general reactions are more likely to be made by key organisational decision-makers who allocate resources for training.

Perceptions of the Value of the Particular Training: In addition to reactions related to the utility or value of training generally, some actors within the organisation will be more concerned with the value of a particular training programme. For example, line managers will have reactions concerning whether the training will lead to performance improvements (Ulrich and Dulebohn 2015), and middle and senior managers will be concerned about whether the training addresses competency and capability gaps.

Course Recommendation Intentions: Training programme reputation is a very important organisation-level reaction to training. For example, Sitzmann and Ely (2011) highlight that the reputation of a training programme is particularly important when it comes to learner choices about participation in training. Research also highlights that the brand reputation of a training programme is particularly important where trainees are viewed as consumers and training as a product (LeBlanc and Nguyen 1996). Reputation of training will be influenced by word of mouth recommendations (Reichheld 2004), therefore course recommendation intentions are an important organisation-level reaction. Howardson and Behrend (2016) highlight that the collective reactions of individuals are important determinants of the overall reputation of a training programme.

Overall within the context of our training effectiveness model, we first differentiate between individual versus organisational-level reactions to training. These individual and organisation-level reactions consist of both cognitive and affective components (Alliger et al. 1997) hence we have modelled them as distinct constructs.

4.6 Learning Outcomes from Training

With our model, we make a clear distinction between trainee reactions and learning outcomes, consistent with the extant literature (Kraiger et al. 1993; Kirkpatrick 1987). Reactions are conceptualised as event or programme perceptions but do not focus on what the trainee has learned as a result of training. Consistent with our overall model, we make a distinction between individual and organisational-level learning outcomes. In the context of our model, we conceptualise individual-level learning outcomes to include: cognitive, skill and affective outcomes. At the organisational level, we identify three types of learning outcomes: (a) socialisation and indoctrination about the importance of training; (b) knowledge about new and continued KSA gaps within the organisation and (c) knowledge about new ways of selecting employees for training.

4.6.1 Individual-Level Learning Outcomes

We conceptualise these learning outcomes as proximal because they are the direct result of participation in the training. Kraiger et al. (1993) make an important differentiation between cognitive, skill-based and attitudinal/motivational learning outcomes. They define cognitive learning outcomes as those concerned with job-related knowledge including declarative, procedural and tacit organisational knowledge and the development of cognitive strategies for problem-solving and decision-making. The skills-based learning outcomes of training focus on behavioural changes, skill acquisition and skill automaticity that is derived from training. Attitudinal outcomes are frequently not given consideration (Sitzmann et al. 2008) but training can lead to important motivational states (Brown 2005). Affective outcomes include attitudinal and motivational components such as self-efficacy, learning motivation, motivation to use training and more general affective outcomes such as job satisfaction, greater job involvement and job engagement. The research is generally agreed that this categorisation of individual learning outcomes represents the full spectrum of outcomes derived from training.

4.6.2 Organisational-Level Learning Outcomes

Our model specifies three categories of organisational-level learning outcomes. The first category of organisational learning outcome focuses on issues related to socialisation and indoctrination related to the importance of training. This outcome will be manifest in positive attitudes about the value of training among employees and managers. This could include agreement about the values of continuous L&D, the development of intentions to engage in future training and development and acceptance of the importance of training (Tracey et al. 1995). The development of positive organisational-level reactions to training will lead to cognitions and attitudes that prioritise training and the development of learning behaviours focused on engagement and participation in training (Maurer and Tarulli 1994). Our second organisational-level learning outcome focuses on knowledge about new and continued KSA gaps that need to be addressed in the organisation. This is an important component of our model because it is a reflection of how well training is done in the organisation and it sets off a further chain of training activity. Managers and first-line supervisors, for example, will be able to make more informed decisions about what skills have improved and further training that is required. Scholars have highlighted the importance of training in developing the collective human capital of the organisation. An important general assumption is that training will produce employees capable of fulfilling the collective human capital needs of the organisation (Dachner et al. 2013). Given that the majority of training activity takes place at the discretion of the employer, through carefully designed training programmes, these collective human capital outcomes are anticipated and expected. Our third category of organisational learning outcome is concerned with knowledge about new ways of selecting and preparing employees for participation in training. For example, organisations will generate insights as to what worked best, how to select trainees to maximise KSA development and collective human capital.

4.7 Learning Transfer—Organisational and Individual Levels

Central to our model is the argument that for training to impact both proximal and distal firm performance outcomes, successful implementation of the training must occur. Successful implementation is conceptualised as the transfer of the training which is defined as the 'extent to which the learning that results from a training programme transfers to the job and leads to meaningful changes in work performance' (Blume et al. 2010: 1066). In the context of our model, we distinguish between individual and organisational level transfer factors. Baldwin and Ford (1988) in his model of training transfer distinguished trainee from organisational factors as key determinants of the transfer process. The research evidence reveals that the level of transfer decreases significantly over time (Blume et al. 2010) and that the environment plays a major role in influencing the continuance of transfer (Dragoni et al. 2014). Hughes et al. (2019) proposed the concept of training sustainment to capture how trained KSAs on the job fluctuate over time. They argue that for training to lead to distal or organisational outcomes, there is a need for prolonged use of trained behaviours on-the-job (Hughes et al.

2019). Our model acknowledges that the transfer process is complex and multi-level (Edmondson et al. 2004) and accordingly considers factors at both levels of analysis.

4.7.1 Trainee Transfer

The trainee transfer component of our model focuses on factors that transfer back to the job. The concept of transfer in the training literature is used in a relatively narrow sense to focus on factors that impact the use of skills on the job (Kirkpatrick 1987). We focus here on three individual-level characteristics—motivation to transfer, self-efficacy to transfer and stable individual characteristics.

Motivation to Transfer: Research has highlighted the particular importance of motivation to transfer (Chiaburu and Lindsay 2008; Holton 1996). Motivation to transfer is conceptualised as the drive or inspiration of an individual to apply knowledge gained through training in a job-specific context (Noe and Schmitt 1986). It is considered a critical component of overall motivation and it influences the amount and quality of training transferred. A variety of individual studies and meta-analyses (Huang et al. 2017; Blume et al. 2010; Hughes et al. 2019) have highlighted the important role of motivation to transfer as a mediator, explaining the positive link between environmental support and the optimal level of transfer.

Self-Efficacy to Transfer: Self-efficacy to transfer has also emerged as an important individual determinant of transfer of training (Gibson 2004; Bandura 1986). It is argued that individuals with high beliefs in their capabilities will approach challenging transfer tasks and maintain sustained efforts to achieve optimum transfer, in particular, where individuals are high on self-efficacy to transfer, they will set self-challenging transfer goals and show greater effort, persistence and task achievement (Guillen and Feltz 2011). Individuals high on self-efficacy are more motivated and committed to transfer skills to the workplace.

Stable Individual Characteristics: Huang et al. (2017) highlight the importance of stable individual differences in the context of transfer. First, they argued and found support for the notion that cognitive ability is a significant predictor of maximum performance outcomes. Therefore, where trainees have the ability and capability to transfer, it should lead to higher levels of transfer. They also identified the important role of conscientiousness where highly conscientious individuals are more motivated and will pursue set goals. Beus and Whitman (2012) found that conscientiousness is associated with high performance. Huang et al. (2017) found that conscientiousness had a mediating role in the context of transfer.

4.7.2 Organisation-Level Transfer

Like training transfer, the organisational-level component is also an important level of analysis in the context of trainer effectiveness. This component, for the purposes of our model, focuses on: (a) organisational learning culture; (b) transfer climate and (c) work environment support variables.

Organisational Learning Culture: Organisational learning culture is conceptualised as a culture that fosters the practices of acquisition of knowledge, its transfer and the recognition for transfer application (Yang et al. 2004). It is argued that the development of such a culture plays a key role in creating a shared consensus among organisational members about the value of training and learning and the use of new skills in the workplace (Watkins 2005). Some researchers have conceptualised organisational learning culture to be multi-dimensional whereas others view it as a holistic, unified concept (Egan et al. 2004). Research evidence is generally supportive of the importance of organisational learning culture in influencing motivation to transfer training (Banerjee et al. 2016).

Learning Transfer Climate: The concept of learning transfer climate is closely related to organisational learning culture (Bates and Khasawneh 2005). However, unlike organisational learning culture, it is viewed as a more visible construct and imitates surface-level manifestations of cultural beliefs. Learning transfer climate as a domain-specific concept emphasises employee perceptions about the existence of a system that encourages sharing of knowledge and skills with organisational members (Ruona et al. 2002). Quratulain et al. (2019) emphasise important features of learning transfer climate. The first dimension, perceived flexibility, emphasises the extent to which the work environment allows employees to work independently, engage in self-directed behaviours and be proactive. The second dimension, performance feedback, highlights feedback as an important resource for employees to apply their learning. In learning transfer climates where there are significant levels of feedback, this gives employees insights into appropriate transfer behaviour and they can make improvements accordingly. There is exclusive research highlighting the importance of learning transfer climate (Blume et al. 2010; Hughes et al. 2019).

Work Environment Supports: Research has also focused on understanding the impact various organisational supports have in fostering training transfer (Cromwell and Kolb 2004). Three forms of support are particularly highlighted: organisational, supervisory and peer support. These various forms of support help employees to utilise strategies to transfer training (Clarke 2003). Supervisory support is considered to be one of the most proximate and critical forms of support (Blume et al. 2010; Van den Bossche and Segers 2013). In particular, it is argued that supervisory support can provide trainees with the required assurance that it is appropriate to engage in training implementation behaviours (Nihman et al. 2006).

4.8 Firm-Level Human Resource Outcomes

We propose within our model that employee transferred KSAs attitudes and behaviours aggregate to become firm-level human resources (Ployhart et al. 2014) and these human resource outcomes have the potential to influence firm operational and financial performance outcomes. In terms of conceptualising these outcomes, we utilise the AMO Model (Kellner et al. 2019) to conceptualise them into ability (A), motivation (M) and opportunity (O) outcomes. An important assumption of the AMO Model is that training will impact firm performance through its impact on the three elements. So to follow this logic further, training will have an effect on collective human capital components such as adaptability, creativity, collective engagement, employee commitment and empowerment. These firm-level collective human capital outcomes lead in turn to operational and then financial outcomes. There is an extensive body of research highlighting these outcomes.

Ability-Focused Outcomes: It is not surprising that researchers have focused to a major degree on ability-based outcomes. These include increased knowledge, skills and experience (Cobblah and Van der Walt 2016), employee competencies, collective human capital (Raineri 2017) and management skills. Ability also includes positive behaviours and job performance. Examples include job performance (Horgan and Muhlau 2006), work effort, work role behaviours (Fletcher 2016), customer-oriented behaviours (Peccei and Rosenthal 2001), knowledge sharing behaviours (Yu et al. 2010), in-role and extra-role behaviours (Tremblay et al. 2010). The literature has also investigated the impact of training on more negative work behaviours such as stress (Okay-Somerville and Scholarios 2019) and employee discipline (Horgan and Muhlau 2006).

Motivation-Focused Outcomes: Researchers have also given considerable focus to a variety of motivation-based outcomes such as organisational commitment (Kooij et al. 2015), employee engagement (Odle-Dusseau et al. 2015), employee loyalty (Hassan et al. 2013) and overall motivation (Wright et al. 2001). Withdrawal behaviour has also emerged as an important motivational component. Examples of dimensions studied include absenteeism/attendance (Kampkotter and Marggraf 2015), turnover rates/quit rates (Shaw et al. 1998), losing employees to competitors (Beynon et al. 2002) and intention to leave/stay (Lam et al. 2002).

Opportunity-Focused Outcomes: Researchers have given very little attention to the investigation of opportunity-based outcomes. Those that have been investigated include opportunities for employee involvement (Odle-Dusseau et al. 2015), helping behaviours (Chaung and Liao 2010) and peer support and relationships (Haung and Hsueh 2007).

Conceptually these firm-level collective human resource outcomes can be understood as human capital resources (Ployhart et al. 2014) which are defined as firm-level capabilities that are accessible for firm performance purposes. In our model, we propose that the availability of these collective human capital resources is influenced by a variety of contextual factors. These contextual factors we describe as emergence enablers that will moderate the extent to which firm-level human capital outcomes lead to operational performance outcomes.

4.9 Emergence Enablers

The concept of emergence enablers is an important idea to help explain how collective human capital leads to operational firm outcomes. Kozlowski and Klein (2000: 55) defined emergent phenomena as constructs that 'originate in the cognition, affect behaviours and other characteristics of individuals, amplified by their interactions and manifest as higher level, collective phenomena(s)'. Investigation of emergent enablers in the context of training effectiveness is relatively nascent. Ployhart and Moliterno (2011) proposed three categories of emergent enablers—cognitive, behavioural and affective. We utilise this categorisation to make sense of the relatively modest literature base.

Cognitive Emergent Enablers: This category of enablers focuses on characteristics such as culture, climate and collective learning processes. Examples of these factors within the literature include learning orientation (Gutiérrez-Gutiérrez et al. 2012), organisational learning processes (Aragon et al. 2014), work climate and environment (Gelade and Ivery 2003), organisational culture (Lau and Ngo 2004), leadership (Burton and O'Reilly 2004) and organisational fairness (Kooij et al. 2013).

Behavioural Emergent Enablers: This category focuses on communication, coordination, collaboration and behavioural processes that impact the interdependencies of employees. Examples of these emergent processes highlighted in the literature include learning by doing (Harel and Tzafrir 1999), knowledge integration (Guiltierrez-Guiltierrez et al. 2012), knowledge sharing (Buch et al. 2015), knowledge management processes (Bhatti et al. 2011) and supervisory coaching (Hamlin et al. 2006).

Affective Emergent Enablers: This category of emergent enabler focuses on the emotional bonds that link employees together such as trust, team cohesion and team processes. Examples of studies that have investigated these factors in the context of training include coworker support (Bashir and Long 2015), perceived supervisory support

(Buch et al. 2015), trust (Gould-Williams 2007), social and economic exchanges (Jung and Takeuchi 2019) and team leadership activities (Santos et al. 2015).

4.10 Operational Firm-Level Outcomes

We specify in our model two additional categories of organisational performance outcomes—operational and financial. Operational firm performance outcomes are conceptualised as distal outcomes; however, they are closely linked with the collective human resource outcomes that we discussed earlier. For the purpose of our model, we identify four categories of operational outcomes: workforce productivity, customer service and service quality, organisational innovation and employee turnover.

Workforce Productivity: One of the most frequently investigated operational outcomes of training is workforce productivity. Examples of dimensions of productivity investigated include subjective productivity (Abdullah et al. 2008), objective workforce productivity (Barrett and O'Connell 2001), employee productivity (Paul and Anantharanman 2003) and productivity (Wickramasinghe and Wickramasinghe 2017) and industry-specific work productivity (Gelade and Ivery 2003).

Customer Service/Product Quality: Researchers have investigated a variety of customer service/product quality operational outcomes. These include customer satisfaction/referrals (Ely 2004), service quality (Glaveli and Karassavidou 2011), service performance (Browning 2006), product quality (Murray and Raffaele 1997), service and product performance (Akhtar et al. 2008), defect density (Appleyard and Brown 2001), customer service effectiveness (Beltrán-Martin and Bou-Llusar 2018), customer satisfaction (Jing et al. 2014), store-level service performance (Liao and Chuang 2004), service quality (Marley et al. 2004), customer handling (Ragg 2011), store image (Russell et al. 1985), calls abandoned (Wood et al. 2006) and customer alignment (Youndt et al. 1997).

Innovation Outcomes: Innovation is also highlighted as an important operational outcome of investment in training. Researchers have investigated a wide variety of innovation types including managers' innovativeness (Aragon and Sanz-Valle 2013), radical and incremental innovation (Beugelsdijk 2008), product and process innovation (Dostie 2018), number of firm patents (Diaz-Fernandez et al. 2015), innovation performance (Chen and Huang 2009), technological and administrative innovation (Kim and Chung 2017), new product development (Lau and Ngo 2004) and organisational improvement (Yazdanfar et al. 2014).

Employee Turnover: Employee turnover represents a negative operational performance outcome of investment in training. Researchers have investigated a number of dimensions of employee turnover; however, the findings are mixed. For example, Aguinis and Kraiger (2009) found that perceived L&D was associated with higher levels of retention and Dysvik and Kuvaas (2008) found that it strengthened the social exchange between employer and employee. Recent studies by Koster et al. (2011) found that its relationship is contingent on job satisfaction and Fletcher et al. (2016) found that employee engagement, job satisfaction and change-related anxiety mediated the relationship between training and intention to stay.

4.11 Financial Performance Outcomes

Financial outcomes are considered one of the most important bottom-line outcomes of investment in training. Researchers have operationalised financial performance in a number of different ways. We identify four categories of financial performance: sales growth, market share, profitability/growth and ROI/ROE. Studies have investigated a variety of measures of sales growth including sales level (Birley and Westhead 1990), sales revenue growth (Altinay et al. 2008), sales per employees (Buck et al. 2003), new sales (Ely 2004), sales growth rate (Lee and Chee 1996), return on sales (Yang et al. 2015) and sales performance relative to competitors (Zakaria et al. 2018).

Profitability/Growth: Researchers have investigated various dimensions of profitability growth including: gross profit (Chatterjee et al. 2018), abnormal returns (Riley et al. 2017), profitability (Aragon-Sanchez et al. 2003), profitability performance growth (Bal and Dorenbosch 2015), annual earnings (Chandler and McEvoy 2000), export growth and export intensity (Deng et al. 2003) and economic profit (Lopez et al. 2005).

Market Performance: Researchers have investigated multiple dimensions of market performance including option value (Berk and Kaše 2010), success index (Glaub et al. 2014), economic performance (Meschi and Metais 1998) and business failure (Burton and O'Reilly 2004).

Return on Investment: Financial measures such as Return on Assets (ROA) and Return on Equity (ROE) feature prominently in the literature. Specific examples include return on capital employed (ROCE) (D'Arcimoles 1997), return on investment (ROI) (Meschi and Metais 1998), ROA (Aragon and Sanz-Valle 2013) and ROE (Darwish et al. 2013).

4.12 Summary

In this chapter we presented the key findings in respect to our model of L&D effectiveness in organisations. The model is informed by open systems thinking and envisages a set of inputs, processes and outcomes. We highlighted three key inputs: environmental and organisational inputs, trainee characteristics inputs and training design inputs. We conceptualised the process components to include: individual and organisational reactions to training, individual and organisational learning outcomes and individual and organisational transfer factors. Our model specified four dimensions related to outcomes: the role of emergence factors, collective human resource outcomes, operational performance outcomes and finally financial outcomes. We proposed that the emergence factors play a role in influencing whether learning outcomes transfer to collective human resource outcomes.

References

Abdullah, M. M. B., Uli, J., & Tarí, J. J. (2008). The influence of soft factors on quality improvement and performance: Perceptions from managers. *Total Quality Management Journal, 20*(5), 436–452.

Aguinis, H., & Kraiger, K. (2009). Benefits of training and development for individuals and teams, organizations, and society. *Annual Review of Psychology, 60*(1), 451–474.

Akhtar, S., Ding, D. Z., & Ge, G. L. (2008). Strategic HRM practices and their impact on company performance in Chinese enterprises. *Human Resource Management, 47*(1), 15–32.

Alliger, G. M., Tannenbaum, S., Bennett, W., Traver, H., & Shotland, A. (1997). A meta-analysis of the relations among training criteria. *Personnel Psychology, 50,* 341–358.

Altinay, L., Altinay, E., & Gannon, J. (2008). Exploring the relationship between the human resource management practices and growth in small service firms. *The Service Industries Journal, 28*(7), 919–937.

Appleyard, M. M., & Brown, C. (2001). Employment practices and semiconductor manufacturing performance. *Industrial Relations, 40*(3), 436–471.

Aragon, M. I. B., Jiménez-Jiménez, D., & Sanz-Valle, R. (2014). Training and performance: The mediating role of organisational learning. *Business Research Quarterly, 17*(3), 161–173.

Aragon, M. I. B., & Sanz-Valle, R. (2013). Does training managers pay off? *The International Journal of Human Resource Management, 24*(8), 1671–1684.

Aragon-Sanchez, A., Aragon, M. I. B., & Sanz-Valle, R. (2003). Effect of training on business results. *International Journal of Human Resource Management, 14*(6), 956–980.

Arthur, W., Jr., Bennett, W., Jr., Edens, P. S., & Bell, S. T. (2003). Effectiveness of training in organizations: A meta-analysis of design and evaluation features. *Journal of Applied Psychology, 88*(2), 234–245.

Aycan, Z., Kanungo, R., Mendonca, M., Yu, K., Deller, J., Stahl, G. et al. (2000). Impact of culture on human resource management practices: A 10-country comparison. *Applied Psychology, 49*(1), 192–221.

Bal, P. M., & Dorenbosch, L. (2015). Age-related differences in the relations between individualised HRM and organisational performance: A large-scale employer survey. *Human Resource Management Journal, 25*(1), 41–61.

Baldwin-Evans, K. (2007). The future of organisational learning. *Industrial and Commercial Training, 39*(6), 299–306.

Baldwin, T. T., & Ford, J. K. (1988). Transfer of training: A review and directions for future research. *Personnel Psychology, 41,* 63–105.

Bandura, A. (1986). *Prentice-Hall series in social learning theory. Social foundations of thought and action: A social cognitive theory*. Upper Saddle River, NJ: Prentice-Hall.

Banerjee, P., Gupta, R., & Bates, R. (2016). Influence of organisational learning culture on knowledge worker's motivation to transfer training: Testing moderating effects of learning transfer climate. *Current Psychology, 36,* 606–617.

Barrett, A., & O'Connell, P. J. (2001). Does training generally work? The returns to in-company training. *Industrial and Labour Relations Review, 54*(3), 642–662.

Barrick, M. R., & Mount, M. K. (1991). The big five personality dimensions and job performance: A meta-analysis. *Personnel Psychology, 44*(1), 1–26.

Barrick, M. R., Stewart, G. L., & Piotrowski, M. (2002). Personality and job performance: Test of the mediating effects of motivation among sales representatives. *Journal of Applied Psychology, 87*(1), 43–51.

Bashir, N., & Long, C. S. (2015). The relationship between training and organisational commitment among academicians in Malaysia. *Journal of Managerial Development, 34*(10), 1227–1245.

Bates, R., & Khasawneh, S. (2005). Organisational learning culture, learning transfer climate and perceived innovation in Jordanian organisations. *International Journal of Training and Development, 9*(2), 96–109.

Beier, M. E., & Kanfer, R. (2010). Motivation in training and development. In S. W. J. Kozlowski & E. Salas (Eds.), *Learning, training, and development in organisations* (pp. 65–97). NY: Psychology Press.

Beltrán-Martin, I., & Bou-Llusar, J. C. (2018). Examining the intermediate role of employee abilities, motivation and opportunities to participate in the relationship between HR bundles and employee performance. *Business Research Quarterly, 21*(2), 99–110.

Berk, A., & Kaše, R. (2010). Establishing the value of flexibility created by training: Applying real options methodology to a single HR practice. *Organization Science, 21*(3), 765–780.

Bettis, R. A., & Hitt, M. A. (1995). The new competitive landscape. *Strategic Management Journal, 16*(1), 7–19.

Beugelsdijk, S. (2008). Strategic human resource practices and product innovation. *Organization Studies, 29,* 821–847.

Beus, J. M., & Whitman, D. S. (2012). The relationship between typical and maximum performance: A meta-analytical examination. *Human Performance, 25*(5), 355–376.

Beynon, H., Grimshaw, D., Rubery, J., & Ward, K. (2002). *Managing employment Change: The new realities of work*. Oxford: Oxford University Press.

Bezrukova, K., Spell, C. S., Perry, J. L., & Jehn, K. A. (2016). *A meta-analytical integration of over 40 years of research on diversity training evaluation.* Available from http://scholarship.sha.cornell.edu/articles/974.

Bhatti, W. A., Zaheer, A., & Rehman, K. (2011). The effect of knowledge management practices on organisational performance: A conceptual study. *African Journal of Business Management, 5,* 2847–2853.

Birley, S., & Westhead, P. (1990). Private business sales environments in the United Kingdom. *Journal of Business Venturing, 5*(6), 349–373.

Birou, L. M., Green, K. W., & Inman, R. A. (2019). Sustainability knowledge and training: Outcomes and firm performance. *Journal of Manufacturing Technology Management, 30*(2), 294–311.

Blanchard, N. P., & Thacker, J. (2007). *Effective training: Systems, strategies, and practices*. London: Pearson.

Blom, R., Kruyen, P. M., Van der Heijden, B., & van Thiel, S. (2018). One HRM fits all: A meta-analysis of the effects of HR practices in the public, semi-public, and private sector. *Review of Public Personnel Administration, 40*(1), 3–35.

Blume, B. D., Ford, J. K., Baldwin, T. T., & Huang, J. L. (2010). Transfer of training: A meta-analytic review. *Journal of Management, 36*(4), 1065–1105.

Boudreau, J. (2016). HR expertise: Facing the future of work. *Society for Human Resource Management*. Available from https://www.shrm.org/hr-today/news/hr-magazine/pages/0116-competencies-hr-expertise-boudreau.aspx.

Brown, K. G. (2005). An examination of the structure and nomological network of trainee reactions: A closer look at "smile sheets". *The Journal of Applied Psychology, 90*(5), 991–1001.

Browning, V. (2006). The relationship between HRM practices and service behaviour in South African service organisations. *International Journal of Human Resource Management, 17*(7), 1321–1338.

Buch, R., Dysvik, A., Kuvaas, B., & Nerstad, C. G. (2015). It takes three to tango: Exploring the interplay among training intensity, job autonomy, and supervisor support in predicting knowledge sharing. *Human Resource Management, 54*(4), 623–635.

Buck, T., Filatotchev, I., Demina, N., & Wright, M. (2003). Inside ownership, human resource strategies and performance in a transition economy. *Journal of International Business Studies, 34,* 530–549.

Budhwar, P. S., & Sparrow, P. R. (2002). An integrative framework for understanding cross-national human resource management practices. *Human Resource Management Review, 12,* 377–403.

Burton, M. D., & O'Reilly, C. (2004). *Walking the talk: The impact of high commitment values and practices on technology start-ups.* Cornell University, School of Industrial and Labor Relations. Available from http://digitalcommons.ilr.cornell.edu/workingpapers/99.

Cambridge Dictionary. (2019). *Definition of 'gig economy'.* Available from https://dictionary.cambridge.org/dictionary/english/gig-economy.

Campbell, J. P. (1988). Training design for performance improvement. In J. P. Campbell & R. J. Campbell (Eds.), *Productivity in organizations* (pp. 177–215). San Francisco, CA: Jossey-Bass.

Cennamo, L., & Gardner, D. (2008). Generational differences in work values, outcomes and person-organisation values fit. *Journal of Managerial Psychology, 23*(8), 891–906.

Cerasoli, C. P., Alliger, G. M., Donsbach, J. S., Mathieu, J. E., Tannenbaum, S. I., & Orvis, K. A. (2018). Antecedents and outcomes of informal learning behaviours: A meta-analysis. *Journal of Business and Psychology, 33*(2), 203–230.

Cervone, D., & Peake, P. K. (1986). Anchoring, efficacy, and action: The influence of judgmental heuristics on self-efficacy judgments and behaviour. *Journal of Personality and Social Psychology, 50*(3), 492–501.

Chadwick, I. C., & Raver, J. L. (2015). Motivating organisations to learn: Goal orientation and the influence of organisational learning. *Journal of Management, 41*(3), 957–986.

Chandler, G. N., & McEvoy, G. M. (2000). Human resource management, TQM, and firm performance in small and medium-size enterprises. *Entrepreneurship: Theory and Practice, 25*(1), 43–57.

Chatterjee, S., Dandapat, D., & Bagchi, B. (2018). *Efficiency of growth drivers: An analysis of select Indian industries.* New York: Springer.

Chen, C. J., & Huang, J. W. (2009). Strategic human resource practices and innovation performance—The mediating role of knowledge management capacity. *Journal of Business Research, 62*(1), 104–114.

Chen, Y., & Jermias, J. (2016). Linking key performance indicators to new international venture survival. *Journal of International Accounting Research, 15*(3), 31–48.

Cheung, F., & Wu, A. M. (2013). Older workers' successful aging and intention to stay. *Journal of Managerial Psychology, 28*(6), 645–660.

Chiaburu, D. S., & Lindsay, D. R. (2008). Can do or will do? The importance of self-efficacy and instrumentality for training transfer. *Human Resource Development International, 11*(2), 199–206.

Clarke, N. (2003). The politics of training needs analysis. *Journal of Workplace Learning, 15*(4), 141–153.

Cobblah, M. C., & Van der Walt, T. B. (2016). Staff training and development programmes and work performance in the university libraries in Ghana. *Information Development, 33*(4), 375–392.

Cohen, D. J. (1990). What motivates trainees? *Training and Development Journal, 44*(11), 91–93.

Collings, D. G., Mellahi, K., & Cascio, W. F. (2019). Global talent management and performance in multinational enterprises: A multilevel perspective. *Journal of Management, 45*(2), 540–566.

Collins, D. B., & Holton, E. F. (2004). The effectiveness of managerial leadership development programs: A meta-analysis of studies from 1982 to 2001. *Human Resource Development Quarterly, 15*(2), 153–170.

Colquitt, J. A., LePine, J. A., & Noe, R. A. (2000). Toward an integrative theory of training motivation: A meta-analytic path analysis of 20 years of research. *Journal of Applied Psychology, 85*(5), 678–707.

Cranny, C. J., Smith, P. C., & Stone, E. (1992). *Job satisfaction: How people feel about their jobs*. Lexington: Lexington Books.

Cromwell, S. E., & Kolb, J. A. (2004). An examination of work-environment support factors affecting transfer of supervisory skills training to the workplace. *Human Resource Development Quarterly, 15*(4), 449–471.

Curado, C., Henriques, P. L., & Ribeiro, S. (2015). Voluntary or mandatory enrolment in training and the motivation to transfer training. *International Journal of Training and Development, 19*(2), 98–109.

D'Arcimoles, C. (1997). Human resource policies and company performance: A quantitative approach using longitudinal data. *Organizational Studies, 18*, 857–874.

D'Souza, C., Kay-Raining Bird, E., & Deacon, H. (2012). Survey of Canadian speech-language pathology service delivery to linguistically diverse clients. *Canadian Journal of Speech-Language Pathology and Audiology, 36*(1), 18–39.

Dachner, A. M., Saxton, B. M., Noe, R. A., & Keeton, K. E. (2013). To infinity and beyond: Using a narrative approach to identify training needs for unknown and dynamic situations. *Human Resource Development Quarterly, 24*(2), 239–267.

Dachner, A. M., Ellingson, J. E., Noe, R., & Saxton, B. M. (2019). The future of employee development. *Human Resource Management Review*. https://doi.org/10.1016/j.hrmr.2019.100732.

Darwish, T. K., Singh, S., & Mohamed, A. F. (2013). The role of strategic HR practices in organisational effectiveness: An empirical investigation in the country of Jordan. *International Journal of Human Resource Management, 24*(17), 3343–3362.

Deng, J., Menguc, B., & Benson, J. (2003). The impact of human resource management on export performance of Chinese manufacturing enterprises. *Thunderbird International Business Review, 45*(4), 409–420.

Denison, D. (1996). What is the difference between organizational culture and organizational climate? A native's point of view on a decade of paradigm wars. *The Academy of Management Review, 21*(3), 619–654.

Diaz-Fernandez, M., Bornay-Barrachina, M., & Lopez-Cabrales, A. (2015). Innovation and firm performance: The role of human resource management practices. *Evidence-Based HRM, 3*(1), 64–80.

Dostie, B. (2018). The impact of training on innovation. *ILR Review, 71*(1), 64–87.

Dragoni, L., Oh, I. S., Tesluk, P. E., Moore, O. A., Van Katwyk, P., & Hazucha, J. (2014). Developing leaders' strategic thinking through global work experience: The moderating role of cultural distance. *Journal of Applied Psychology, 99*(5), 867–882.

Dulebohn, J. H., & Johnson, R. D. (2013). Human resource metrics and decision support: A classification framework. *Human Resource Management Review, 23*(1), 71–83.

Dysvik, A., & Kuvaas, B. (2008). The relationship between perceived training opportunities, work motivation and employee outcomes. *International Journal of Training and Development, 12*(3), 138–157.

Edmondson, A. C., Kramer, R. M., & Cook, K. S. (2004). Psychological safety, trust and learning in organizations: A group-level lens. *Trust and Distrust in Organizations: Dilemmas and Approaches, 12,* 239–272.

Egan, T. M., Yang, B., & Bartlett, K. R. (2004). The effects of organizational learning culture and job satisfaction on motivation to transfer learning and turnover intention. *Human Resource Development Quarterly, 15*(3), 279–301.

Ely, R. (2004). A field study of group diversity, participation in diversity education programs, and performance. *Journal of Organizational Behaviour, 25,* 755–780.

Farndale, E., Scullion, H., & Sparrow, P. (2010). The role of the corporate HR function in global talent management. *Journal of World Business, 45*(2), 161–168.

Fletcher, L. (2016). Training perceptions, engagement, and performance: Comparing work engagement and personal role engagement. *Human Resource Development International, 19*(1), 4–26.

Fletcher, L., Alfes, K., & Robinson, D. (2016). The relationship between perceived training and development and employee retention: The mediating role of work attitudes. *International Journal of Human Resource Management, 29*(18), 2701–2728.

Gallup. (2018). *Put the gig economy to work for you.* Available from https://www.gallup.com/workplace/240878/gig-economy-paper-2018.aspx.

Garavan, T. N., Heneghan, S., O'Brien, F., Gubbins, C., Lai, Y., Carbery, R. et al. (2019). L&D professionals in organisations: Much ambition, unfulfilled promise. *European Journal of Training & Development, 44*(1), 1–86.

Garavan, T., McCarthy, A., Lai, Y., Murphy, K., Sheehan, M., & Carbery, R. (2020). Training and organisational performance: A meta-analysis of temporal, institutional, and organisational context moderators. *Human Resource Management Journal*, in-press.

Garavan, T. N., Shanahan, V., Carbery, R., & Watson, S. (2016). Strategic human resource development: Towards a conceptual framework to understand its contribution to dynamic capabilities. *Human Resource Development International, 19*(4), 289–306.

Gelade, G. A., & Ivery, M. (2003). The impact of human resource management and work climate on organizational performance. *Personnel Psychology, 56*, 383–404.

Giangreco, M. F., Suter, J. C., & Doyle, M. B. (2010). Paraprofessionals in inclusive schools: A review of recent research. *Journal of Educational and Psychological Consultation, 20*(1), 41–57.

Gibson, S. K. (2004). Social learning (cognitive) theory and implications for human resource development. *Advances in Developing Resources, 6*(2), 193–210.

Gist, M. E., Stevens, C. K., & Bavetta, A. G. (1991). Effects of self-efficacy and post-training intervention on the acquisition and maintenance of complex interpersonal skills. *Personnel Psychology, 44*, 837–861.

Glaub, M. E., Frese, M., Fischer, S., & Hoppe, M. (2014). Increasing personal initiative in small business managers or owners leads to entrepreneurial success: A theory-based controlled randomized field intervention for evidence-based management. *Academy of Management Learning & Education, 13*(3), 354–379.

Glaveli, N., & Karassavidou, E. (2011). Exploring a possible route through which training affects organizational performance: The case of a Greek bank. *The International Journal of Human Resource Management, 22*(14), 2892–2923.

Gould-Williams, J. (2007). HR practices, organizational climate and employee outcomes: evaluating social exchange relationships in local government. *The International Journal of Human Resource Management, 18*(9), 1627–1647.

Gu, Z., & Chi Sen Siu, R. (2009). Drivers of job satisfaction as related to work performance in Macao casino hotels: An investigation based on employee survey. *International Journal of Contemporary Hospitality Management, 21*(5), 561–578.

Gubbins, C., & Garavan, T. (2009). Understanding the HRD role in MNCs: The imperatives of social capital and networking. *Human Resource Development Review, 8*(2), 245–275.

Guerrero, L., & Posthuma, R. A. (2014). Perceptions and behaviours of hispanic workers: A review. *Journal of Managerial Psychology, 29*(6), 3–33.

Guerrero, S., & Sire, B. (2001). Motivation to train from the workers' perspective: Example of French companies. *The International Journal of Human Resource Management, 12*(6), 988–1004.

Guillen, F., & Feltz, D. (2011). A conceptual model of referee efficacy. *Frontiers in Psychology, 2*(25), 1–5.

Gusdorf, M. L. (2009) *Training design, development and implementation.* Society of Human Resource Management, 1–34.

Gutiérrez-Gutiérrez, L. J., Bustinza, O. F., & Barrales-Moline, V. (2012). Six sigma, absorptive capacity and organisational learning orientation. *International Journal of Production Research, 50*(3), 661–675.

Hamlin, R. G., Ellinger, A. D., & Beattie, R. S. (2006). Coaching at the heart of managerial effectiveness: A Cross-cultural study of managerial behaviours. *Human Resource Development International, 9*(3), 305–331.

Harel, G. H., & Tzafrir, S. S. (1999). The effect of human resource management practices on the perceptions of organizational and market performance of the firm. *Human Resource Management, 38*(3), 185–199.

Hassan, M. G., Hassan, S., Khan, M. F. A., & Iqbal, A. (2013). Impact of HR practices on employee satisfaction and employee loyalty: An empirical study of government owned public sector banks of Pakistan. *Middle East Journal of Scientific Research, 16*(1), 1–8.

Holton, E. F., III. (1996). The flawed four level evaluation model. *Human Resource Development Quarterly, 7,* 5–21.

Horgan, J., & Muhlau, P. (2006). Human resource systems and employee performance in Ireland and the Netherlands: A test of the complementarity hypothesis. *International Journal of Human Resource Management, 17*(3), 414–439.

Howardson, G. N., & Behrend, T. S. (2016). Coming full circle with reactions: Understanding the structure and correlates of trainee reactions through the affect circumplex. *Academy of Management Learning & Education, 15*(3), 471–492.

Huang, J. L., Ford, J. K., & Ryan, A. M. (2017). Ignored no more: Within-person variability enables better understanding of training transfer. *Personal Psychology, 70,* 557–596.

Huang, C., & Hsueh, S. (2007). A study of the relationship between intellectual capital and business performance in the engineering consulting industry: A path analysis. *Journal of Civil Engineering and Management, 4,* 265–271.

Hughes, A., Zajac, S., Woods, A. L., & Salas, E. (2019). The role of work environment in training sustainment: A meta-analysis. *Human Factors, 62*(1), 166–183.

Hurtz, G. M., & Williams, K. J. (2009). Attitudinal and motivational antecedents of participation in voluntary employee development activities. *Journal of Applied Psychology, 94*(3), 635–653.

Isenhour, L. C., Stone, D. L., & Lien, D. (2012). Advancing theory and research on employee behaviour in China. *Journal of Managerial Psychology, 27*(1), 4–8.

Jarrahi, M. H. (2018). Artificial intelligence and the future of work: Human-AI symbiosis in organisational decision making. *Business Horizons, 61*(4), 577–586.

Jing, F. F., Avery, G. C., & Bergsteiner, H. (2014). Enhancing performance in small professional firms through vision communication and sharing. *Asian Pacific Journal of Management, 31,* 599–620.

Jung, Y., & Takeuchi, N. (2019). Testing mediation effects of social and economic exchange in linking organizational training investment to employee outcomes. *Personnel Review, 48*(2), 306–323.

Kalinoski, Z. T., Steele-Johnson, D., Peyton, E. J., Leas, K. A., Steinke, J., & Bowling, N. A. (2013). A meta-analytic evaluation of diversity training outcomes. *Journal of Organizational Behaviour, 34*(8), 1076–1104.

Kampkotter, P., & Marggraf, K. (2015). Do employees reciprocate to intra-firm trainings? An analysis of absenteeism and turnover rates. *International Journal of Human Resource Management, 26*(22), 2888–2907.

Kanfer, R., & Ackerman, P. L. (1989). Motivation and cognitive abilities: An integrative-aptitude-treatment interaction approach to skill acquisition. *Journal of Applied Psychology, 74*, 657–690.

Karasek, R., & Theorell, T. (1990). *Healthy work: Stress, productivity, and the reconstruction of working life*. New York: Basic Books.

Kellner, A. K., Cafferkey, K., & Townsend, K. (2019). Ability, motivation and opportunity theory: A formula for employee performance. In *Introduction to Theories of Human Resource Management*. Cheltenham: Edward Elgar Publishing.

Kim, J., & Chung, G. H. (2017). Implementing innovations within organisations: A systematic review and research agenda. *Innovation: Organisation & Management, 19*(3), 372–399.

Kim, Y., & Ployhart, R. E. (2014). The effects of staffing and training on firm productivity and profit growth before, during and after the Great Recession. *Journal of Applied Psychology, 99*(3), 361–389.

Kirkpatrick, D. L. (1987). Evaluation of training. In R. L. Craig (Ed.), *Training and development handbook: A guide to human resource development* (pp. 301–319). New York: McGraw-Hill.

Kooij, D., Guest, D., Clinton, M., Knight, T., Jansen, P., & Dikkers, J. (2013). How the impact of HR practices on employee well-being and performance changes with age? *Human Resource Management Journal, 23*(1), 18–35.

Kooij, D., Tims, M., & Kanfer, R. (2015). Successful aging at work: The role of job crafting. In P. M. Ball, T. A. M. Kooij, & D. M. Rousseau (Eds.), *Aging workers and the employee-employer relationship* (pp. 145–161). Switzerland: Springer.

Koster, F., De Grip, A., & Fouarge, D. (2011). Does perceived support in employee development affect personnel turnover? *International Journal of Human Resource Management, 22*(11), 2403–2418.

Kozlowski, S. W. J., & Klein, K. J. (2000). A multilevel approach to theory and research in organizations: Contextual, temporal, and emergent processes. In K. J. Klein & S. W. J. Kozlowski (Eds.), *Multilevel theory, research and methods in organizations: foundations, extensions, and new directions* (pp. 3–90). San Francisco, CA: Jossey-Bass.

KPMG. (2016). *Global HR transformation report*. Available from https://assets.kpmg/content/dam/kpmg/pdf/2016/06/fr-hr-transformation.pdf.

Kraiger, K., Ford, J. K., & Salas, E. (1993). Application of cognitive, skill-based and affective theories of learning outcomes to new methods of training evaluation. *Journal of Applied Psychology, 78,* 311–328.

Lacerenza, C. N., Reyes, D. L., Marlow, S. L., Joseph, D. L., & Salas, E. (2017). Leadership training design, delivery, and implementation: A meta-analysis. *Journal of Applied Psychology, 102*(12), 1686–1718.

Lam, T., Lo, A., & Chan, J. (2002). New employees' turnover intentions and organizational commitment in the Hong Kong hotel industry. *Journal of Hospitality & Tourism Research, 26*(3), 217–234.

Lau, C. M., & Ngo, H. Y. (2004). The HR system, organisational culture, and product innovation. *International Business Review, 13*(6), 685–703.

LeBlanc, G., & Nguyen, N. (1996). Cues used by customers evaluating corporate image in service firms: An empirical study in financial institutions. *International Journal of Service Industry Management, 7*(2), 44–56.

Lee, M. B., & Chee, Y. (1996). Business strategy, participative human resource management and organizational performance: The case of South Korea. *Asia Pacific Journal of Human Resources, 34,* 77–94.

Lee, T. D., & Genovese, E. D. (1988). Distribution of practice in motor skill acquisition: Learning and performance effects reconsidered. *Research Quarterly for Exercise and Sport, 59*(4), 277–287.

Liao, H., & Chuang, A. (2004). A multilevel investigation of factors influencing employee service performance and customer outcomes. *The Academy of Management Journal, 47*(1), 41–58.

Loon, M. (2016). Confluent learning in developing change management capabilities. *Journal of Organizational Behaviour Education, 9,* 83–104.

Lopez, S. P., Montes-Peon, J. M., & Vazquez-Ordas, C. J. (2005). Organisational learning as a determining factor in business performance. *The Learning Organisation, 12*(3), 227–245.

Magerko, B., Wray, B., Holt, L., & Stensrud, B. (2005). *Improving interactive training through individualised content and increased engagement*. Industry Training, Simulation and Education Conference.

Marley, K. A., Collier, D. A., & Goldstein, S. M. (2004). The role of clinical and process quality in achieving patient satisfaction in hospitals. *Decision Sciences, 35*(3), 349–360.

Martinez-Sanchez, A., Perez-Perez, M., de-Luis, P., & Véla-Jiménez, M. J. (2007). Teleworking and workplace flexibility: A study of impact on firm performance. *Personnel Review, 36*(1), 42–64.

Mathieu, J. E., & Martineau, J. W. (1997). Individual and situational influences in training motivation. In J. K. Ford, S. W. J. Kozlowski, K. Kraiger,

E. Salas, & M. S. Teachout (Eds.), *Improving training effectiveness in organizations* (pp. 193–222). Hillsdale, NJ: Erlbaum.

Mathieu, J. E., Martineau, J. W., & Tannenbaum, S. I. (1993). Individual and situational influences on the development of self-efficacy: Implications for training effectiveness. *Personnel Psychology, 46,* 125–147.

Maurer, T. J., & Tarulli, B. A. (1994). Investigation of perceived environment, perceived outcome, and person variables in relationship to voluntary development activity by employees. *Journal of Applied Psychology, 79*(1), 3–14.

McCormick, M. J. (2000). *The influence of goal-orientation and sex-role identity on the development of leadership self-efficacy during a training intervention.* Doctoral dissertation, retrieved from ProQuest Dissertations & Theses (9957488).

McKinsey Global Institute. (2017). *Jobs lost, jobs gained: Workforce transitions in a time of automation.* New York: McKinsey & Company.

McNamara, T. K., Parry, E., Lee, J., & Pitt-Catsouphes, M. (2011). The effect of training on organisational performance: Differences by age composition and cultural context. *The International Journal of Human Resource Management, 23*(6), 1226–1244.

Menzel, N., & Gutierrez de Blume, A. P. (2010). Latino workers perceptions of construction risks. *American Journal of Industrial Medicine, 53*(2), 179–187.

Meschi, P., & Metais, E. (1998). A socio-economic study of companies through their training policies: New empirical considerations in the French context. *MIR: Management International Review, 38*(1), 25–48.

Miles, R. E., Snow, C. C., Meyer, A. D., & Coleman, H. J. (1978). Organisational strategy, structure, and process. *The Academy of Management Review, 3*(3), 546–562.

Morgan, R. B., & Casper, W. J. (2000). Examining the factor structure of participant reactions to training: A multidimensional approach. *Human Resource Development Quarterly, 11*(3), 301–317.

Murray, B., & Raffaele, G. C. (1997). Single-site, results-level evaluation of quality awareness training. *Human Resource Development Quarterly, 8*(3), 229–245.

Nadiv, R., Raz, A., & Kuna, S. (2017). What a difference a role makes: Occupational and organizational characteristics related to the HR strategic role among human resource managers. *Employee Relations, 39*(7), 1131–1147.

Nihman, D. J. M., Nijhof, W. J., & Veldkamp, B. P. (2006). Exploring differential effects of supervisor support on transfer of training. *Journal of European Industrial Training, 30*(7), 529–549.

Noe, R. A. (1986). Trainees' attributes and attitudes: Neglected influences on training effectiveness. *Academy of Management Review, 11*(4), 736–749.

Noe, R. (2017). *Employee training and development*. New York, NY: McGraw Hill Education.

Noe, R. A., & Schmitt, N. (1986). The influence of trainee attitudes on training effectiveness: Test of a model. *Personnel Psychology, 39*, 497–523.

Odle-Dusseau, H. N., Hammer, L. B., Crain, T., & Bodner, T. E. (2015). The influence of family-supportive supervisor training on employee job performance and attitudes: An organizational work-family intervention. *Journal of Occupational Health Psychology, 21*(3), 296–308.

Okay-Somerville, B., & Scholarios, D. (2019). A multilevel examination of skills-oriented human resource management and perceived skill utilization during recession: Implications for the well-being of all workers. *Human Resource Management, 58*(2), 139–154.

Paas, F., Renkl, A., & Sweller, J. (2004). Cognitive load theory: Instructional implications of the interaction between information structures and cognitive architecture. *Instructional Science, 32*(1), 1–8.

Paluck, E. L. (2006). Diversity training and intergroup contact: A call to action research. *Journal of Social Issues, 62*(3), 577–595.

Paul, A. K., & Anantharaman, R. N. (2003). Impact of people management practices on organizational performance: Analysis of a causal model. *The International Journal of Human Resource Management, 14*(7), 1246–1266.

Peccei, R., & Rosenthal, R. (2001). Delivering customer-oriented behaviour through empowerment: An empirical test of HRM assumptions. *Journal of Management Studies, 38*(6), 831–857.

Phillips, J. M., & Gully, S. M. (1997). Role of goal orientation, ability, need for achievement, and locus of control in the self-efficacy and goal–setting process. *Journal of Applied Psychology, 82*(5), 792–802.

Ployhart, R. E., & Moliterno, T. P. (2011). Emergence of the human capital resource: A multi-level model. *The Academy of Management Review, 36*(1), 127–150.

Ployhart, R. E., Nyberg, A. J., Reilly, G., & Maltarich, M. A. (2014). Human capital is dead; long live human capital resources! *Journal of Management, 40*, 371–398.

Quinn, J. B., Anderson, P., & Finkelstein, S. (1997). Managing professional intellect: Making the most of the best. *The Strategic Management of Intellectual Capital*, 87–98.

Quratulain, S., Khan, A. K., Sabharwal, M., & Javed, B. (2019). Effect of self-efficacy and instrumentality beliefs on training implementation behaviours:

Testing the moderating effect of organisational climate. *Review of Public Personnel Administration*, in-press.
Ragg, M. (2011). *Developing practice competencies: A foundation for generalist practice*. Hoboken, NJ: Wiley.
Raemdonck, I., Gijbels, D., & van Groen, W. (2014). The influence of job characteristics and self-directed learning orientation on workplace learning. *International Journal of Training and Development, 18*(3), 188–203.
Raineri, A. (2017). Linking human resources practices with performance: the simultaneous mediation of collective affective commitment and human capital. *The International Journal of Human Resource Management, 28*(22), 3149–3178.
Rauch, A., & Hatak, I. (2016). A meta-analysis of different HR-enhancing practices and performance of small and medium sized firms. *Journal of Business Venturing, 31*(5), 485–504.
Rehmann, A. J., Mitman, R. D., & Reynolds, M. C. (1995). *A handbook of flight simulation fidelity requirements for human factors research*. Federal Aviation Administration Technical Center.
Reichheld, F. F. (2004). The one number you need to grow. *Harvard Business Review, 81*(12), 46–54.
Ricceri, F. (2008). *Intellectual capital and knowledge management: Strategic management of knowledge resources*. London: Routledge.
Richard, P. J., Devinney, T. M., Yip, G. S., & Johnson, G. (2009). Measuring organisational performance: Towards methodological best practice. *Journal of Management, 35*(3), 718–804.
Riley, S. M., Michael, S. C., & Mahoney, J. T. (2017). Human capital matters: Market valuation of firm investments in training and the role of complementary assets. *Strategic Management Journal, 38*(9), 1895–1914.
Rosenthal, P., Hill, S., & Peccei, R. (1997). Checking out service: Evaluating excellence, HRM and TQM. *Work, Employment & Society, 11*(3), 481–503.
Ruona, W. E., Leimback, M., Holton III, E. F., & Bates, R. (2002). The relationship between learner utility reactions and predicted learning transfer among trainees. *International Journal of Training and Development, 6*(4), 218–228.
Russ-Eft, D., & Preskill, H. (2005). In search of the Holy Grail: Return on investment evaluation in human resource development. *Advances in Developing Human Resources, 7*(1), 71–85.
Russell, J. S., Terborg, J. R., & Powers, M. L. (1985). Organisational performance and organisational level training and support. *Personnel Psychology, 38*(4), 849–863.

Sahinidis, A. G., & Bouris, J. (2008). Employee perceived training effectiveness relationship to employee attitudes. *Journal of European Industrial Training, 32*(1), 63–76.

Salas, E., & Cannon-Bowers, J. A. (2001). The science of training: A decade of progress. *Annual Review of Psychology, 52,* 471–499.

Salas, E., DeRouin, R. E., & Littrell, L. N. (2005). Research-based guidelines for designing distance learning: What we know so far. In H. G. Guetal & D. L. Stone (Eds.), *The brave new world of eHR: Human resource management in the digital age* (pp. 104–137). San Francisco, CA: Jossey-Bass.

Salas, E., Shuffler, M. L., Thayer, A. L., Bedwell, W. L., & Lazzara, E. H. (2015). Understanding and improving teamwork in organizations: A scientifically-based practical guide. *Human Resource Management, 54,* 599–622.

Santos, J. P., Caetano, A., & Tavares, S. M. (2015). Is training leaders in functional leadership a useful tool for improving the performance of leadership functions and team effectiveness? *The Leadership Quarterly, 26*(3), 470–484.

Schmidt, S. W. (2010). The relationship between job training and job satisfaction: A review of the literature. *International Journal of Adult Vocational Education and Technology, 1*(2), 19–28.

Schwab, K. (2016). *The fourth industrial revolution.* Geneva, Switzerland: World Economic Forum.

Scott-Jackson, W., Owens, S., Saldana, M., Charles, L., Green, M., Woodman, P. et al. (2016). *Learning to Lead*. London: Chartered Management Institute.

Sebastiano, A., & Bellet, I. (2005). Continuous professional development in healthcare companies: The critical aspects of the training process. *Sanità Pubblica E Privata, 2,* 29–39.

Seijts, G. H., Latham, G. P., Tasa, K., & Latham, B. W. (2004). Goal-setting and goal orientation: An integration of two different yet related literatures. *Academy of Management Journal, 47*(2), 227–239.

Shaw, J. D., Delery, J. E., Jenkins, G. D., & Gupta, N. (1998). An organizational-level analysis of voluntary and involuntary turnover. *Academy of Management Journal, 41,* 511–525.

Sitzmann, T., & Ely, K. (2011). A meta-analysis of self-regulated learning in work-related training and educational attainment: What we know and where we need to go. *Psychological Bulletin, 137,* 421–442.

Sitzmann, T., & Johnson, S. K. (2012). When is ignorance bliss? The effects of inaccurate self-assessments of knowledge on learning and attrition. *Organisational Behaviour and Human Decision Processes, 117*(1), 192–207.

Sitzmann, T., & Weinhardt, J. M. (2015). Training engagement theory: A multilevel perspective on the effectiveness of work-related training. *Journal of Management, 44*(2), 732–756.

Sitzmann, T., Brown, K. G., Casper, W. J., Ely, K., & Zimmerman, R. D. (2008). A review and meta-analysis of the nomological network of trainee reactions. *Journal of Applied Psychology, 93*(2), 280–295.

Snow, C. C., & Hrebiniak, L. G. (1980). Strategy, distinctive competence, and organisational performance. *Administrative Science Quarterly, 25*(2), 317–336.

Sparrow, P. (2007). *Globalisation of HR at function level: Exploring the issues through international recruitment, selection and assessment processes*. CAHRS Working Paper Series, 457.

Stone, D. L., & Deadrick, D. L. (2015). Challenges and opportunities affecting the future of human resource management. *Human Resource Management Review, 25*(2), 139–145.

Stone-Romero, E. F., Stone, D. L., & Hyatt, D. (2003). Personnel selection procedures and invasion of privacy. *Journal of Social Issues, 59*(2), 343–368.

Tan, J., Hall, R. J., & Boyce, C. (2003). The role of employee reactions in predicting training effectiveness. *Human Resource Development Quarterly, 14*(4), 397–411.

Tapscott, D. (2009). *Grown up digital: How the net generation is changing your world*. New York: McGraw-Hill.

Teckchandani, A., & Schultz, F. C. (2014). The vision thing: An experiential exercise introducing the key activities performed by leaders. *Journal of Leadership Studies, 8*(1), 63–70.

Tharenou, P. (2001). The relationship of training motivation to participation in training and development. *Journal of Occupational and Organisational Psychology, 74*(5), 599–621.

Tracey, J. B., Tannenbaum, S. I., & Kavanaugh, M. J. (1995). Applying trained skills on the job: The importance of the work environment. *Journal of Applied Psychology, 80*, 239–252.

Tremblay, M., Cloutier, J., Simard, G., Chenevert, D., & Vandenberghe, C. (2010). The role of HRM practices, procedural justice, organizational support and trust in organizational commitment and in-role and extra-role performance. *The International Journal of Human Resource Management, 21*(3), 405–433.

Twenge, J. M., Campbell, S. M., Hoffman, B. J., & Lance, C. E. (2010). Generational differences in work values: Leisure and extrinsic values increasing, social and intrinsic values decreasing. *Journal of Management, 36,* 1117–1142.

Tzabbar, D., Tzafrir, S., & Baruch, Y. (2017). A bridge over troubled water: Replication, integration and extension of the relationship between HRM practices and organisational performance using moderating meta-analysis. *Human Resource Management Review, 27*(1), 134–148.

Tziner, A., Fisher, M., Senior, T., & Weisberg, J. (2007). Effects of trainee characteristics on training effectiveness. *International Journal of Selection and Assessment, 15*(2), 167–174.

Ulrich, D., & Dulebohn, J. (2015). Are we there yet? What's next for HR? *Human Resource Management Review, 25,* 188–204.

Van den Bossche, P., & Segers, M. R. (2013). Transfer of training: Adding insight through social network analysis. *Educational Research Review, 8,* 37–47.

Vandewalle, D., Cron, W. L., & Slocum, J. (2001). The role of goal orientation following performance feedback. *Journal of Applied Psychology, 86*(4), 629–640.

Vancouver, J. B., Weinhardt, J. M., & Vigo, R. (2014). Change one can believe in: Adding Learning to Computational Models of self-regulation. *Organisational Behaviour and Human Decision Making, 124*, 56–74.

Wang, Z., Yang, B., & McLean, G. N. (2007). Influence of demographic factors and ownership type upon organizational learning culture in Chinese enterprises. *International Journal of Training and Development, 11*(3), 154–165.

Warr, P., & Bunce, D. (1995). Trainee characteristics and the outcomes of open learning. *Personnel Psychology, 48,* 347–375.

Watkins, C. (2005). Classrooms as learning communities: A review of research. *London Review of Education, 3*(1), 47–64.

West, D. M. (2018). *The future of work: Robots, AI, and automation.* Washington, DC: Brookings Institution Press.

White, D. S., Gunasekaran, A., & Ariguzo, G. C. (2012). The structural components of a knowledge-based economy. *International Journal of Business Innovation and Research, 7*(4), 504–518.

Wickramasinghe, V., & Wickramasinghe, G. L. D. (2017). Autonomy support, need fulfilment and job performance in lean implemented textile and apparel firms. *Research Journal of Textile and Apparel, 21*(4), 323–341.

Wood, S., Holman, D., & Stride, C. (2006). Human resource management and performance in UK call centres. *British Journal of Industrial Relations, 44*(1), 99–124.

Wright, P. M., Dunford, B. B., & Snell, S. A. (2001). Human resources and the resource-based view of the firm. *Journal of Management, 27*(6), 701–721.

Yang, B., Watkins, K. E., & Marsick, V. J. (2004). The construct of the learning organization: Dimensions, measurement, and validation. *Human Resource Development Quarterly, 15*(1), 31–55.

Yang, T., Xun, J., & He, X. (2015). British SMEs' e-commerce technological investments and firm performance: An RBV perspective. *Technology Analysis & Strategic Management, 27*(5), 586–603.

Yazdanfar, D., Abbasian, S., & Hellgren, C. (2014). Competence development and performance among Swedish micro firms. *European Journal of Training and Development, 38*(3), 162–179.

Youndt, M. A., Snell, S. A., Dean, J. W., & Lepak, D. P. (1997). Human resource management, manufacturing strategy, and firm performance. *Academy of Management Journal, 39*(4), 836–866.

Yu, T. K., Lu, L. C., & Liu, T. S. (2010). Exploring factors that influence knowledge sharing behaviour via weblogs. *Computers in Human Behaviour, 26*(1), 32–41.

Zakaria, N., Fauzi, W. I. M., Abdullah, N. A. C., & Yusoff, R. Z. (2018). The link between HRM practices and performance in Malaysian SMEs. *International Journal of Supply Chain Management, 7*(6), 118–126.

5

The Current State of Research on Training Effectiveness

Abstract This chapter addresses the current state of research on training effectiveness in organisations. It summarises the key findings on what we know about training effectiveness, the research emphasis given to different components of the model, and how research informs the ways in which organisations should approach learning and development to maximise effectiveness. The chapter highlights the role of training needs analysis, the types of attendance policies that should be used, the most effective design of training delivery to maximise effectiveness, the relative effectiveness of training methods, the organisation of training content, the importance of learning or training transfer, and the types of outcomes that are derived from learning and development.

Keywords State of learning and development effectiveness research · Key research findings on effectiveness · Evidence of best practice approaches to learning and development

T. N. Garavan et al.
Learning and Development Effectiveness in Organisations,
https://doi.org/10.1007/978-3-030-48900-7_5

5.1 Introduction

We stared this monograph by arguing that while business leaders and L&D practitioners attach great value to investment in L&D and are continually focused on finding out what training and development practices work best; researchers have paid insufficient attention to what works best in practice. Our aim in this monograph was to bridge this gap between theory and practice and enhance our understanding of the complexity and dynamics of training effectiveness in practice. Throughout Chapter 4 we have built up and explained the various components of our training effectiveness model. In this, our second to last chapter, we seek to answer the following questions: (a) what do we know about the effectiveness of each component of our integrated model? (b) what particular emphasis has been given to different dimensions of our model in the literature? (c) what are the most important and impactful aspects of training effectiveness? and (d) how should one design, deliver and implement training programmes in organisations to maximise training effectiveness?

5.2 What Do We Know About the Effectiveness of Each Component of Our Integrated Model?

Overall, our review of the literature highlights that researchers have contributed important knowledge and insights to our understanding of the effectiveness of training in organisations. This suggests that, contrary to popular opinion, there is value in utilising training to achieve important firm performance outcomes. Specifically, the current review of the literature highlights that training where it is effectively designed, can lead to important firm outcomes. However, our review reveals that insufficient attention has been given to exploring the relationships in our model, therefore, we discuss each component separately at a theoretical level, while conscious that each are integrated and mediated.

We were, however, able to identify some bivariate relationships among the various components of our model. Therefore, we coded each relationship as part of this review and then computed an average sample-weighted correlation for each potential relationship investigated, where there were at least two samples. Our findings are presented in Fig. 5.1.

These bivariate findings, in general, reveal modest positive relationships between different components of the model and provide some support for the critical explanations of linkages between components of the model. While the estimates are, in some cases, based on small samples of studies—they are in the main based on cross-sectional single-source data—they merit being reported because they suggest evidence of linkages and provide the basis for future research. Our preliminary analysis suggests a number of interesting relationships:

- Environmental inputs are potentially related to organisational reactions to training ($r = .18$) however, the sample of studies is very small;
- Organisational inputs including strategy, culture, L&D strategy and HR practices are linked to learner reactions to training ($r = .26$), organisational reactions to training ($r = .27$) and organisational transfer factors ($r = .21$);
- Individual learner inputs in the form of human capital, demographic and motivational characteristics are linked to learner reactions to training ($r = .31$) and individual learning outcomes ($r = .14$);
- Training design inputs in the form of type of training, duration, trainer learning objects, etc., are positively linked to learner reactions to training ($r = .36$), individual learning outcomes ($r = .34$) and learner transfer characteristics ($r- = .21$);
- Learner reactions to training are positively linked to individual learning outcomes ($r = .37$) and learner transfer characteristics ($r = .31$). In turn individual learning outcomes are positively linked to learning transfer characteristics ($r = .27$). Learner transfer characteristics are positively linked to human resource outcomes ($r = .27$) and organisational transfer characteristics are also positively linked to human resource outcomes ($r = .21$).

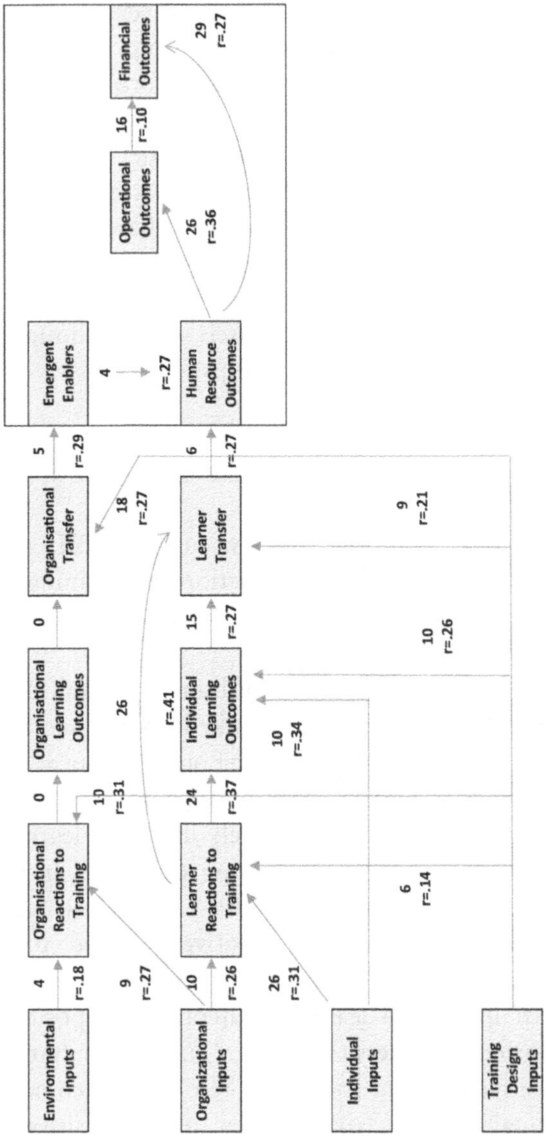

Fig. 5.1 Average Bivariate Correlations between Different Variables within our Model

- In terms of the financial components of our model, human resource outcomes are positively linked to operational outcomes (r = .36) and financial outcomes (r = .10). Emergent enablers are positively linked to human resource outcomes (r = .27), however, the numbers of samples are small. Finally, operational outcomes are positively linked to financial outcomes (r = .27).

Overall, this review does indicate that training is effective in terms of enhancing individual and organisational reactions to training, individual learning outcomes, individual transfer characteristics, human resource outcomes, operational and financial outcomes. Of particular significance is that these results reveal that firm-level outcomes are derived as a result of investment in training. Our findings in particular suggest that there is a chain linking human resource outcomes to operational and then financial outcomes. This therefore suggests an important trickle-up effect (individual-level outcomes aggregated to the firm level). This is an important finding because it is supported in the human capital literature, whereby it is argued that individual-level human capital outcomes lead to organisational-level human capital outcomes. The extent to which this is possible may be contingent on the role of emergent enablers, however, the research base on this issue is very modest indeed. This suggests that future research should achieve a greater understanding of these links.

5.3 What Emphasis Has Been Given to Different Components of Our Model?

Table 5.1 provides a comprehensive summary of how the various components have been studied in the literature. It is very clear from our review that there is a very significant level of unequal empirical attention given to the key components we highlighted.

Inputs: First, there is relatively limited attention given to the role of environmental inputs and their impact on organisational-level reactions to training and organisational transfer characteristics. Researchers have given more attention to the investigation of organisational inputs and their impacts on other components of the model. The research

Table 5.1 Summary of Training Effectiveness Research by Model Component

Model Component and Sub-Category	*Variables and Sample Research*
Environmental /Organisational Inputs:	
Globalisation	• Cross-country difference (Ahmad and Schroeder 2003) • Internationalisation (Deng et al. 2003) • Export intensity (Beugelsdijk 2008) • National culture or cross-cultural difference (Cho and Yoon 2009) • FDI status (Chi et al. 2008) • Country of origin (Kown and Rupp 2013) • Globalisation (Kumar and Lui 2005) • Market competitiveness (Delaney and Huselid 1996) • Industrial market (Aragon-Sanchez et al. 2003) • Market growth (Gooderham et al. 2006) • Business environment (Harel and Tzafrir 1999) • Industrial productivity (Kaminski 2001) • Economic condition (Kim and Ployhart 2014) • Customer affluence (Litz and Stewart 2000) • Market uncertainty (Millier and Lee 2001) • Market demand (Sung and Choi 2012) • Market change (Sung and Choi 2014) • Shifts from manufacturing to service (Stone and Deadrick 2015) • Changes in the knowledge and skill requirements (Stone and Deadrick 2015)
Workforce Diversity	• Age diversity and training preferences (Kraiger and Ford 2007) • Generational differences and preferences for training approaches and methods (Lowell and Morris 2019)

Model Component and Sub-Category	*Variables and Sample Research*
Changing Technology	• Role of interactive technologies to deliver training (Howard and Gutworth 2020)
	• Use of technology for decision making about training (Lux et al. 2007)
	• The impact of technology on training delivery (Cascio 2000)
Changing Job Skills	• Millennial attitudes and training (Beinicke and Bipp 2018)
	• The training issues related to the gig economy (CIPD 2017)
Industry Growth and Sector	• Sector (public vs private sector, Harel and Tzafrir 1999; public sector only; Gould-Williams 2007)
	• For profit-making industry only (Chowhan 2016)
	• For manufacturing vs non-manufacturing (Jimenez-Jimenez and Sanz-Valle 2005)
	• Specific sector (e.g., manufacturing, Abdullah et al. 2008; non-manufacturing industry, Dermol and Cater 2013)
	• Specific industry (e.g. banking industry, Glaveli and Karassavidou 2011)
	• R&D capital (Ballot et al. 2006)
	• Physical capital (Riley et al. 2017)
	• Investment in fixed assets (Barrett and O'Connell 2001)
	• Technology investment/capital (Berk and Kaše 2010)
	• Materials capital (Boon and van der Eijken 1997)
	• Capital intensity (Koch and McGrath 1996)
	• Training grants from external source (Holzer et al. 1993)
	• E-commerce/IT budget (Yang et al. 2015)

(continued)

Table 5.1 (continued)

Model Component and Sub-Category	*Variables and Sample Research*
Firm Size	• Organisation size (Horgan and Muhlau 2006; small firms only Altinay et al. 2008) • Union density/influence (Tzafrir 2005) • Single or multiple establishment (Black and Lynch 1996) • Family ownership (Aragon-Sanchez et al. 2003) • Hierarchical levels (Beugelsdijk 2008) • Workforce characteristics (e.g. % of female workers, age composition, Jiang et al. 2012; % of part-time and temporary staff, Gooderham et al. 2006)
Business Strategy and Structure	• Innovation strategy (Aragon-Sanchez et al. 2003) • Knowledge strategy (Arunprasad 2017) • Strategic integration or fit (Audea et al. 2005) • Business strategy (Birley and Westhead 1990) • Strategic orientation towards HR (Cho and Yoon 2009) • Marketing strategy (Liao and Chuang 2004) • Strategic flexibility (Gutiérrez-Gutiérrez et al. 2012) • HRM strategy (Horgan and Muhlau 2006) • HRD/training strategy (Ubeda-Garcia et al. 2013) • CSR (Liu et al. 2014) • Information processing and decision-making strategy (Miller and Lee 2001) • Role of training above and beyond other HR practices (Kooij et al. 2013)
Technology & Knowledge Intensity	• Technology intensity (Diaz-Fernandez et al. 2015) • Technological capability (Chatterjee et al. 2018) • Degree of technology newness (Koch and McGrath 1996) • Technological change (Sung and Choi 2014)

Model Component and Sub-Category	*Variables and Sample Research*
Organisation Culture, Climate and Rewards	• Training culture (Sitzman and Weinhardt 2015) • Training culture and skills implementation (Tracey et al. 1995) • Training rewards and engagement (Hurtz and Williams 2009)
Characteristics of the L&D Function and Link with HR	• Complementariness between training and other HR practices (Buch et al. 2015) • HR strength (Guan and Frenkel 2018) • General HR capability and commitment (Karami et al. 2008) • Presence of HR department (Wickramasinghe and Liyanage 2013)
Individual Trainee Inputs	
Trainee Abilities, Knowledge, Dispositions and Values	• Trainee age, education level and occupation (Salas et al. 2012) • Employee skills (Katou et al. 2014) • Employee/managers' ability (Aragon and Sanz-Valle 2013) • Human capital (Berk and Kaše 2010) • Owners' expertise (Chinomona 2013) • Employee competency (Otoo 2019) • Self-efficacy (Glaub et al. 2014) • Education level (Shen and Tang 2018) • Job readiness (Heyler and Lee 2014) • Entrepreneurial business experience (Pratono and Mahmood 2016) • Cultural values and learning (Yang et al. 2004) • Cognitive ability and learning (Colquitt et al. 2000)
Trainee Motivation, Self-Efficacy, Instrumentality & Goals	• Self-efficacy and training instrumentality (Bhatti et al. 2011) • Mastery goals and learning (Grossman and Salas 2011)

(continued)

Table 5.1 (continued)

Model Component and Sub-Category	*Variables and Sample Research*
Trainee Characteristics and Level within the Organisation	• Gender (Akrofi 2016) • Age (Nasurdin et al. 2014) • Job tenure (Bell and Grushecky 2006) • Organisational tenure (Buch et al. 2014) • Job groups (Birdi et al. 2007) • Working hours (Boselie and Paauwe 2005) • Job contract (Piaralal et al. 2014) • Marital status (Georgellis et al. 2012) • Wage (Tessema and Soeters 2006)
Trainee Affective & Behavioural Characteristics	• Trainee emotional exhaustion and job satisfaction (Fletcher et al. 2016) • Organisational/employee commitment (Zhang 2004) • Employees/managers' motivation (Tessema and Soeters 2006) • Employee loyalty (Glaveli and Karassavidou 2011) • Employee satisfaction (Feng et al. 2014) • Work engagement, personal role engagement (Fletcher et al. 2016) • Felt obligation (Frenkel and Bednall 2016) • Employee enthusiasm (Park and Jacobs 2011) • Learning and performance goal orientations (Unger et al. 2011)
Training Design Inputs	
Needs Analysis Process	• Quality of needs analysis process (Lacerenza et al. 2017) • Pre training information and participation in training (Kodwani 2017) • Extensiveness of the training needs analysis (Kodwani and Prashar 2019)
Training Attendance Policy	• Mandatory versus voluntary attendance in leadership development programmes (Lacerenza et al. 2017) • Mandatory versus voluntary in diversity training (Bezrukova et al. 2016)

Model Component and Sub-Category	*Variables and Sample Research*
Training Design Characteristics	• Training on job skills and multi-functions (Ahmad and Schroeder 2003) • On-the-job and off-the-job training (Aragon-Sanchez et al. 2003) • General and specific training (Arunprasad 2017) • Transformational leadership training (Barling et al. 1996) • Team training and cross training (Cappelli and Neumark 2001) • Management development/training (Cjoi and Dickson 2009) • Service related training (Ellinger et al. 2003) • Internal and external training (Laursen and Foss 2003) • Training extensiveness/intensity (Gurbuz and Mert 2011)) • Training emphasis/importance (Cho and Yoon 2009) • Training dedication and commitment (Aragon and Sanz-Valle 2013) • Total expenditure on training (Diaz-Fernandez et al. 2015) • The ratio of total expenditure on training to total payroll/sales (Barrett and O'Connell 2001) • Investment in training (Berk and Kaše 2010) • Number of employees trained (Harel and Tzafrir 1999) • Percentage of employees trained (Esteban-Lloret et al. 2016) • Training hours (Cho and Yoon 2009) • Training days (McNamara et al. 2011) • Percentage of training hours during or outside working hours (Aragon-Sanchez et al. 2003) • Training benefits (Dhar 2015) • Improvement in knowledge (Birou et al. 2019) • Training effectiveness (Delaney and Huselids 1996)

(continued)

Table 5.1 (continued)

Model Component and Sub-Category	*Variables and Sample Research*
	• Training evaluation (Úbeda-García 2005) • Executive and top management team (Akrofi 2016) • Managerial job group (Birley and Westhead 1990) • Proliferation of technology based training in organisations (Sitzmann et al. 2006) • Training instructor characteristics • Customisation of training (Gainey and Klass 2003) • Internal versus external trainers (Kitching and Blackburn 2002) • Value of external trainers (Cooke et al. 2007)
Learner Reactions to Training	
Cognitive Reactions to Training	• Training efficiency, usefulness and trainer performance (Giangreco et al. 2010) • Trainee cognitive reactions are strongly related to learning (Tan et al. 2003) • Trainee reactions to training as a moderator between motivation and training effectiveness (Kodwani and Prashar 2019) • Instrumentality versus behavioural versus affective reactions (Tan et al. 2003) • Affective reactions span from positive to negative (Howardson and Behrend 2016) • Strong relationship between affective reactions and level of learning (Tan et al. 2003) • Satisfaction reactions to training (Howardson and Behrend 2016) • Programme length influenced trainees overall satisfaction reactions to training (Giangreco et al. 2010)
Organisational Reactions to Training	• Managers act as powerful socialisation agendas for training (Aquinis and Kraiger 2009)

Model Component and Sub-Category	*Variables and Sample Research*
Organisational Stakeholders Perceptions of the Value of Training	• Organisational actors form attitudes to overall value of training based on feedback from training courses (Garavan et al. 2020) • Organisational stakeholder reactions impact the availability of resources for training (Sahoo and Mishra 2019)
Perceptions of the Value of the Particular Training Programme	• Organisational actors in particular supervisors and line managers, develop reactions to the value of particular training programmes (Garavan et al. 2020)
Course Recommendation Intentions	• Course recommendation intentions an important component of course reputation (LeBlanc and Nguyen 1996) • Training programmes viewed as products and learners as consumers
Individual Learning Outcomes	
Cognitive Outcomes of Training	• Cognitive outcomes are an inevitable learning outcome of training programmes (Kraiger et al. 1993)
Skill-Based Learning Outcomes of Training	• Skill-based outcomes take longer to achieve (Kraiger et al. 1993) • Skill-based outcomes are dependent on opportunities for practice and rehearsal (Ellis et al. 2005)
Attitudinal /Motivational Learning Outcomes	• Affective learning outcomes are strongly influenced by positive reactions (Sitzmann et al. 2006)
Organisational Learning Outcomes	
Socialisation /Indoctrination of the Importance of Training in Organisations	• No direct research findings however theory suggests this is potentially an outcomes (Kraiger et al. 1993)
Knowledge about New and Continued KSA Requirements	• Research on training needs analysis and feedback from participants highlights this as a possibility (Lacerenza et al. 2017)
Knowledge about Ways of Selecting and Preparing Employees for Participation in Training	• Not yet investigated but knowledge accumulated from delivery of training can enhance selection processes

(continued)

Table 5.1 (continued)

Model Component and Sub-Category	*Variables and Sample Research*
Individual Level Transfer	
Motivation to Transfer	• Motivation to transfer training (Hughes et al. 2019)
Self-Efficacy to Transfer	• Self-efficacy for transfer of public sector employees (Quratulain et al. 2019)
Stable Individual Characteristics and Transfer	• Cognitive ability and transfer (Huang et al. 2017) • Conscientiousness as a personality trait (Huang et al. 2017)
Organisational-Level Transfer	
Organisational Learning Culture	• Organisational learning culture and transfer (Banerjee et al. 2016) • Attitudes to training (Sahoo and Mishra 2019)
Learning Transfer Climate	• Learning transfer climate and work environment (Holton et al. 2000) • Organisational climate and transfer (Quratulain et al. 2019) • Quality of training transfer climate (Kodwani 2017)
Work Environment	• Multiple work environment support dimensions (peer, top and supervisory support) (Hughes et al. 2019)
Human Capital Resources	• Management skills (Audea et al. 2005) • Increased knowledge, skills and experience (Cobblah and Van der Walt 2016) • Employee competency (Gupta-Potnuru and Sahoo 2016) • Human capital (Raineri 2017)
Ability-Based Outcomes	• Job performance (Horgan and Muhlau 2006) • Work effort (Buch et al. 2015) • Work role behaviours (Fletcher et al. 2016) • Knowledge sharing behaviours (Liu and Liu 2011) • Customer-oriented behaviours (Peccei and Rosenthal 2001) • In-role and extra-role behaviours (Tremblay et al. 2010) • Stress & quality of life (Okay-Somerville and Scholarios 2019) • Employee discipline (Horgan and Muhlau 2006)

Model Component and Sub-Category	*Variables and Sample Research*
Motivation-Based Outcomes	• Organisational commitment (Kooij et al. 2013) • Job satisfaction (Garcia García-Bernal et al. 2005) • Employee involvement/engagement (Odle-Dusseau et al. 2015) Organisational commitment and loyalty (Hassan et al. 2013) • Motivation (Wright et al. 2001) • Absenteeism/attendance (Kampkotter and Marggraf 2015) • Turnover rate/quit rate (Shaw et al. 1998) • Losing employees to competitors (Beynon et al. 2002) • Intention to leave/stay (Lam et al. 2002) • OCBs (Gavino et al. 2012)
Emergent Enablers	
Cognitive: Culture, Climate and Leadership	• Transformational leadership (Barling et al. 1996) • Work climate/environment (Gelade and Ivery 2003) • Supportive leader/manager/supervisors (Coetzee et al. 2014) • Highly committed leaders (Burton and O'Reilly 2004) • Social exchange, economic exchange (Jung and Takeuchi 2019) • Organisational fairness (Kooij et al. 2013) • Organisation culture (Lau and Ngo 2004) • *Team leadership function (Santos et al. 2015)* • Procedural justice (Tremblay et al. 2010)
Affective: Trust, Teamwork and Collaboration	• Co-worker supports (Bashir and Long 2015) • Perceived supervisor support (Buch et al. 2015) • Supervisor coaching (Ellinger et al. 2003) • Team process/work (Ely 2004) • Trust (Gould-Williams 2007)

(continued)

Table 5.1 (continued)

Model Component and Sub-Category	*Variables and Sample Research*
Behavioural: Organisational Learning and Knowledge Sharing	• Organisational learning (Aragon et al. 2014) • Learning orientation (Gutiérrez-Gutiérrez et al. 2012) • Learning by doing (Harel and Tzafrir 1999) • Knowledge management (Bhatti et al. 2011) • Knowledge sharing (Buch et al. 2015) • Knowledge integration (Gutiérrez-Gutiérrez et al. 2012)
Operational Outcomes	
Workplace Productivity	• Combined HR outcomes (Ubeda-Garcia et al. 2013) • Subjective labour productivity (Abdullah et al. 2008) • Objective labour productivity (Birdi et al. 2007)
Customer Service and Product Quality	• Customer satisfaction/referrals (Ely 2004) • Product quality (Murray and Raffaele 1997) • Service quality (Glaveli and Karassavidou 2011) • Service performance (Browning 2006)
Organisational Innovation	• Managers' innovativeness (Aragon and Sanz-Valle 2013) • Radical and incremental innovation (Beugelsdijk 2008) • Number of firm patents (Diaz-Fernandez et al. 2015) • Product/process innovation (Dostie 2018) • Technological and administrative innovation (Jiang et al. 2012)
Employee Turnover	• Higher levels of retention (Aguinis and Kraiger 2009) • Training and turnover interventions of employees (Dysvik and Kuvaas 2008) • Training and intention to stay (Fletcher et al. 2016)
Financial Outcomes	
Sales Growth	• Sales level (Birley and Westhead 1990) • Sales/revenue growth (Altinay et al. 2008)

Model Component and Sub-Category	*Variables and Sample Research*
Profitability Growth	• Profitability (Aragon-Sanchez et al. 2003)
	• Gross profit (Chatterjee et al. 2018)
	• Abnormal returns (Riley et al. 2017)
Market Performance	• Option value (Berk and Kaše 2010)
	• Failure & IPO (Burton and O'Reilly 2004)
	• Success index (Glaub et al. 2014)
	• Economic performance (Meschi and Metais 1998)
ROA/ROE	• ROA/ROE (Cho and Yoon 2009)
	• ROA & ROE (Darwish et al. 2013)
	• Return on investment (Meschi and Metais 1998)
	• Return on capital employed (D'Arcimoles 1997)

suggests that organisational inputs are important for both individual and organisational reactions to training, in addition to organisational transfer characteristics. There is more research investigating the role of both individual and training design inputs. Individual inputs have their primary impact on individual earners; however, training design inputs have impacts on both individual and organisational-level factors. These findings highlight the important role that effectively designed training has on the sequences of individual reactions, learning and transfer characteristics, as well as organisational reactions to training and transfer characteristics.

Learner and Organisational Reactions: Secondly, we found that research on individual learner reactions to training has grown significantly in the past 20 years, and it is an important component of our model in terms of explaining learning outcomes and transfer. The investigation of organisational reactions to learning is largely non-existent and there is little in the way of investigations that link individual reactions to organisational training reactions. The investigation of organisational reactions to training is a priority for future researchers and it should focus specifically on how organisational actors react to training activities in general, in addition to reactions to specific programmes of training.

Learner and Organisational Learning Outcomes: Thirdly, our review points to a significant imbalance in terms of the investigation of individual and organisational learning outcomes. The majority of the existing empirical investigations have focused on individual learning outcomes, no doubt influenced by Kirkpatrick (1987). At the same time, little attention has been paid to learning outcomes that organisations derive as a result of training. More research needs to be directed at conceptualising the types of organisational learning that are derived from investment in training. We define these learning outcomes as enhanced knowledge about what works and does not work when it comes to training positioning the selection of participants, the new skill gaps as well as those continuing gaps that arise from providing training and the indoctrination value of training for creating positive attitudes to training generally within the organisation. These types of learning outcomes are not typically examined as outcomes of training but which as per our integrated model, have implications for organisational transfer factors and firm-level performance outcomes.

Individual and Organisational Transfer Characteristics: Fourth, our review suggests a somewhat different story when it comes to the investigation of individual and organisational transfer characteristics. Significant emphasis has been given to both individual and organisation characteristics and their interaction. The significant body of empirical findings is consistent with the theoretical importance give to these dimensions in the literature and their role in our model. We suggest that these transfer characteristics will mediate the relationships between individual and organisational learning and firm-level performance outcomes. Regarding individual-level characteristics, studies have focused on a relatively narrow range of individual stable characteristics, motivations and self-efficacy. In terms of organisational characteristics, researchers have primarily focused on climate and organisational support dimensions. The findings on these dimensions are convincing and have stood the rigors of meta-analyses. The overall assumption of these transfer literature is that where these factors are positive it will lead to enhanced firm-level outcomes; however, this is largely an untested assumption in the literature.

Firm-Level Outcomes: The fifth key finding from our review of the literature concerns firm-level performance outcomes. Overall, these dimensions of outcomes have been extensively studied with major growth in the literature since 2010. This growth is particularly noticeable in the investigation of human resource, operational and financial performance outcomes. Its increased prominence in the literature can largely be attributed to the importance attached to strategic HRM (Garavan et al. 2020). At the same time, there is one major gap at the firm level and this concerns the role of emergent enablers. Further research needs to greatly increase the volume of research on understanding how different categories of emergent enablers (cognitive, behavioural and affective) impact human resource outcomes, which we conceptualise as aggregated individual-level outcomes. Our model particularly specifies that these emergent enablers will act as moderators between the transfer factors and human resource outcomes.

The Most Impactful Components of the Model: So far we have highlighted the prevalence of empirical research on each component of the model. However, the question remains as to which dimensions or components are most impactful for training effectiveness. Our empirical review highlights that training design inputs have a very significant impact on other components of the model. The research essentially suggests that where design components are effectively executed this will lead to a sequence of positive cognitive, affective and satisfaction reactions that then lead to positive learning outcomes on transfer. On the other hand, our review provides very few insights on how these training design inputs impact the organisational-level sequence in our model. Second, the review points to the particular salience of both individual and organisational transfer factors. These components are particularly impactful in providing a bridge to firm-level performance outcomes. Our review shows that organisational-level transfer characteristics assume greater importance than individual-level outcomes in explaining linkages with human resource outcomes. Finally, at the firm level, our conceptual model points to the role of emergent enabler. Research points to the potential role of emergent enablers in helping individual-level outcomes become firm-level outcomes. However, their role is not well understood, thus highlighting a clear need for future research to try and link specific emergent processes with human resource outcomes.

5.4 How Should Organisations Approach the Design, Delivery and Implementation of Training to Maximise Training Effectiveness?

To address this complex question, we rely on the findings generally from our review of empirical studies. We are therefore initially selective in the types of factors that we can address. Table 5.2 provided a detailed summary of meta-analysis findings however we summarise some important key findings here.

Table 5.2 Best available evidence on training effectiveness in organisations: Summary of key findings from meta-analyses

Designing Training Programmes
Best Available Evidence Findings: • In designing behaviour modelling training (BMT), the use of retention aids and displaying learning points along with modelling may hinder learning (Taylor et al. 2005) • In designing BMT, symbolic (mental) rehearsal of skills before behaviour rehearsal led to higher levels of skill development (Taylor et al. 2005) • In designing BMT, transfer of training (effect of training on job behaviour) was largest when at least some of the scenarios that trainees practiced were trainee generated (Taylor et al. 2005) • In designing BMT, training transfer in the form of changes in job behaviour were larger for programmes where trainees set goals, when trainees managers were also trained and when rewards and sanctions were instituted in trainees' workplaces for using/not using newly learned skills (Taylor et al. 2005) • More practice in the form of longer training courses led to greater development of procedural knowledge-skills ($\delta = 0.42$) but had no effect on training transfer in the form of changes in job behaviour (Taylor et al. 2005) • Mixed behaviour modelling training (where both positive and negative instances pertaining to a concept were modelled) had smaller effects on the development of declarative knowledge and change in attitudes than positive only models (Taylor et al. 2005) • Mixed behaviour modelling training showed greater transfer of training in terms of changes in job behaviour than did positive only training modelling (Taylor et al. 2005) • Training that includes **both** cognitive and interpersonal skills or tasks had the largest effects on learning (mean *ds* 2.08) and behavioural criteria (mean *ds* 0.75) followed by psychomotor skills or tasks on learning (mean *ds* 0.80) and behavioural criteria (mean *ds* 0.71). The largest effects on results criteria were from training on interpersonal skills or tasks (mean d 0.88) followed by cognitive skills or tasks (mean ds 0.60) and the smallest for psychomotor skills (mean 0.43) (Arthur et al. 2003) • Leadership training programs that included a needs analysis displayed significantly stronger effects for *learning* ($t = 2.57$) and *transfer* ($t = 16.14$) outcomes than no needs analysis. No difference was found for *results* outcomes (Lacerenza et al. 2017)

(continued)

Table 5.2 (continued)

Designing Training Programmes
• Instructor style and human interaction are strong predictors of reactions but weak predictors of cognitive learning outcomes (Meta-analytic evidence from Sitzmann et al. 2008) • Leadership programs delivered via internal instructors displayed significantly stronger effects for *learning* than those that were self-administered ($t = 2.12$). There was no difference on *learning* between programs delivered by internal or external instructors or self-administered as compared to external instructors (Lacerenza et al. 2017) • Leadership programs delivered via external instructors displayed significantly stronger effects for *transfer* than those that were self-administered ($t = 3.72$). There was no difference on *transfer* between programs delivered by internal instructors as compared to self-administered or by external instructors as compared to internal instructors (Lacerenza et al. 2017) • No difference was found for *results* outcomes for leadership programs delivered by internal or external instructor or self-administered (Lacerenza et al. 2017) • Training for simple skills is more effective when spaced over time than massed in one session (Donovan and Radosevich 1999) • Leadership training programs that spanned across multiple sessions displayed significantly larger effect sizes than training programs based on one massed sessions, for *results* ($t = 5.26$) and *transfer* ($t = 2.28$) (Lacerenza et al. 2017) • Leadership training programs conducted on-site displayed significantly stronger effects for *results* than programs completed off site ($t = 4.17$). No significant differences are found between on and off-site for *learning* or *transfer* (Lacerenza et al. 2017) • Leadership training programs which used practice-based methods exhibited significantly stronger effects on results than information-based methods (Lacerenza et al. 2017) • Leadership training programs incorporating information, demonstration and practice-based methods displayed significantly larger effect sizes for *results* than programs incorporating only information ($t = 2.52$) based methods. No other differences were found for *results* (Lacerenza et al. 2017) • There was no significant difference between leadership training programs using feedback and not using feedback on *results* (Lacerenza et al. 2017) • Leadership training programs conducted on-site displayed significantly stronger effects for *results* than programs completed off site ($t = 4.17$) (Lacerenza et al. 2017)

Designing Training Programmes
• Involuntary leadership programs exhibited significantly stronger effects for *results* outcomes than voluntary programs ($t = 5.30$) (Lacerenza et al. 2017) • Leadership training program duration displayed a significant positive relationship with *results* ($\beta = 0.32$) (Lacerenza et al. 2017) • Organisations that emphasise training quantity (time $\beta = -0.12$, percentage of employees trained $\beta = 0.05$, training expenditure $\beta = -0.11$) performed as well as those whom emphasised training quality (importance given to training, training effectiveness) (Garavan et al. 2020) **Use of Training Methods** *Best Available Evidence Findings:* • Practice is important in both web-based and classroom-based instruction and particularly so for web-based instruction. Web-based instruction is 12% more effective than classroom instruction for teaching declarative knowledge when it incorporates practice (Kulik and Kulik 1991) • Web-based instruction is also more effective than classroom instruction when both delivery formats include practice. However, web based instruction is less effective than classroom instruction when it does not include practice and the classroom based instruction does (Kulik and Kulik 1991) • The level of human interaction in web-based instruction does not impact how much students learn by comparison to classroom instruction which naturally includes human interaction. However, the use of synchronous communication facilitates learning more than asynchronous communication (Kulik and Kulik 1991) • Web-based instruction trainees learnt more than classroom based trainees when they are given a high rather than low level of control (extent to which trainees have control over their learning experience by affecting content, sequence or pace of material) during the training experience (Kulik and Kulik 1991) • Provision of feedback is beneficial for both web-based and classroom-based instruction (Kulik and Kulik 1991) • Web-based instruction trainees gained more declarative knowledge by comparison to classroom based trainees as the length of a training programme increased (Kulik and Kulik 1991)

(continued)

Table 5.2 (continued)

Designing Training Programmes
• To design more effective web-based courses, design conditions to implement include providing trainees with control, practice on the training material, feedback and longer courses. With these design features in place, web-based instruction is 19% more effective than classroom instruction. Classroom instruction is 20% more effective than web-based instruction if web-based instruction does not implement these design features (Kulik and Kulik 1991) • Computer- based instruction is slightly more effective than traditional instruction (Kulik and Kulik 1991) • Web based instruction is 6% more effective than classroom instruction for teaching *declarative* knowledge. Web based instruction and classroom instruction equally effective at teaching *procedural* knowledge (Sitzmann 2011) • Classroom instruction which is supplemented with web based instruction (blended learning) is 13% more effective than classroom instruction alone for teaching declarative knowledge and 20% more effective for teaching procedural knowledge. Blended learning has the instructional advantages of both web- based and classroom instruction and meets individual learner needs by employing multiple delivery media (Sitzmann 2011) • Classroom instruction is more effective than web-based instruction for teaching declarative knowledge when trainee evaluations are based on trainees whom were not permitted to self-select onto courses i.e. choosing whether to do a classroom or web-based course but rather were assigned (Sitzmann 2011) • Educational theory suggests the medium for instruction is less critical in determining learning outcomes than the events of instruction. When the same instructional methods are used web based and classroom instruction are equally effective (Sitzmann 2011) • Trainees receiving instruction via a simulation game had 11% higher declarative knowledge ($d = .28$), 14% higher procedural knowledge ($d = .37$) and 9% higher retention levels ($d = .22$) than trainees in the comparison (no-training group or group whom received training via another instructional method) group (Sitzmann 2011) • When the majority of the instruction in the simulation game is active, the simulation game group learned more than the comparison (no-training group or group whom received training via another instructional method) group ($d = .49$). Whereas if the simulation game passively conveys instructional material, the comparison group learn more ($d = -.11$) (Sitzmann 2011)

Designing Training Programmes
• When simulation games were used as a supplement to other instructional methods, the simulation game group had higher knowledge levels than the comparison group (d = .51) (no-training group or group whom received training via another instructional method). However, when simulation games were used as a standalone instruction, trainees in the comparison group learned more than trainees in the simulation game group (d = −.12) (Sitzmann 2011) • The comparison group (no-training group or group whom received training via another instructional method) learned more than the simulation game group when the comparison group was taught with active instructional methods (e.g. discussion) (d = −.19). However, the simulation game group learned more than the comparison group when the comparison group was taught with passive instructional methods (d = .38) or a combination of lecture and active instructional methods (d = .38) Sitzmann 2011) • Computerised tutorial were more effective than simulation games (d = −.70). (Sitzmann 2011) • Hands-on-practice were slightly more effective than simulation games (d = −.13) (Sitzmann 2011) • Simulation games were more effective than assignments (d = .86) (Sitzmann 2011) • Simulation games were more effective than lecture (d = .45) and reading (d = .42). (Sitzmann 2011) • Leadership training programs which used information-based methods exhibited significantly stronger effects for *learning* than those using practice-based methods (t = 2.24). However, for *results,* practice-based methods exhibited significantly stronger effects than information-based methods (Lacerenza et al. 2017) • Leadership training programs incorporating information, demonstration and practice-based methods displayed significantly larger effect sizes for *learning* than programs incorporating only information (t = 3.15) or practice-based methods (t = 8.32). Leadership training programs incorporating all three training methods of information, demonstration and practice displayed significantly larger effect sizes for *learning* than those incorporating both information and practice-based methods (t = 3.93) (Lacerenza et al. 2017) • The comparison group (no-training group or group whom received training via another instructional method) learned more than the simulation game group when the comparison group was taught with active instructional methods (e.g. discussion) (d = −.19). However, the simulation game group learned more than the comparison group when the comparison group was taught with passive instructional methods (d = .38) or a combination of lecture and active instructional methods (d = .38) (Sitzmann 2011)

(continued)

Table 5.2 (continued)

Designing Training Programmes
• Computerised tutorial were more effective than simulation games ($d = -.70$) (Sitzmann 2011) • Hands-on-practice were slightly more effective than simulation games ($d = -.13$) (Sitzmann 2011) • Simulation games were more effective than assignments ($d = .86$) (Sitzmann 2011) • Simulation games were more effective than lecture ($d = .45$) and reading ($d = .42$). The largest effect sizes on **learning** criterion for **psychomotor** skills or tasks were from the training methods of audio-visual & discussion (mean ds 1.11), lecture, audio-visual (mean ds 0.69) (Sitzmann 2011) • Virtual reality training programmes perform better than alternative approaches to training in developing employees social skills. Gamified training produced poorer results than non- gamified training and programmes using immersive technologies were marginally less effective that programmes using non-immersive displays (Howard and Gutworth 2020)
Determinants of Reactions and Learning Outcomes
Best Available Evidence Findings:
• Intrinsic motivation has the largest relative positive impact on training programme evaluation reactions followed by task value and motivation to transfer. However, practitioners are advised to focus on motivation to learn (meta-analytic evidence from Bauer et al. 2016) • Pre-training motivation positively impacted reactions (Sitzmann et al. 2008) • Trainee characteristics moderately impact reactions. Specifically, pre-training motivation and trainee agreeableness positively impacted reactions and anxiety negatively impacted reactions (Sitzmann et al. 2008) • •Situational characteristics impact reactions. Specifically, instructor style, human interaction and organisational support positively impact reactions. Characteristics of the training course (i.e. instructor style and human interaction are the strongest predictors of reactions. In courses aimed at changing affective outcomes such as motivation or attitudes e.g. towards diversity, then attention should be paid to programme design features such as instructor and student interaction (Sitzmann et al. 2008) • Leadership training programs that included a needs analysis displayed significantly stronger effects for *learning* ($t = 2.57$) outcomes than no needs analysis (Lacerenza et al. 2017)

Designing Training Programmes
• Leadership training programs which used information-based methods exhibited significantly stronger effects for *learning* than those using practice-based methods ($t = 2.24$) (Lacerenza et al. 2017) • Leadership training programs incorporating information, demonstration and practice-based methods displayed significantly larger effect sizes for *learning* than programs incorporating only information ($t = 3.15$) or practice-based methods ($t = 8.32$). Leadership training programs incorporating all three training methods of information, demonstration and practice displayed significantly larger effect sizes for *learning* than those incorporating both information and practice-based methods ($t = 3.93$) (Lacerenza et al. 2017) • Leadership programs delivered via internal instructors displayed significantly stronger effects for *learning* than those that were self-administered ($t = 2.12$). There was no difference on *learning* between programs delivered by internal or external instructors or self-administered as compared to external instructors (Lacerenza et al. 2017) • Programs incorporating business competencies displayed greater effects on *learning* than those incorporating interpersonal or intrapersonal (Lacerenza et al. 2017) • If learning measures are difficult to collect- post-training self -efficacy measures could be used as these are a better predictor of post training immediate and delayed procedural knowledge than reaction measures. (Meta-analytic evidence from Sitzmann et al. 2008) • Behaviour modelling supervisory training positively and most strongly effects (generally large effects) declarative ($\delta = 1.20$) and procedural knowledge and skills ($\delta = 1.18$) (trainees improved by 1 standard deviation) (Taylor et al. 2005) • BMT supervisory training modestly effects attitudes ($\delta = 0.33$) (Taylor et al. 2005) • BMT supervisory training has a small positive effect on job behaviour ($\delta = 0.27$) (Taylor et al. 2005) • BMT has a small positive effect on results pertaining to workgroup productivity ($\delta = 0.13$) and climate ($\delta = 0.11$) (Taylor et al. 2005) • BMT effects on the development of procedural knowledge-skills for technical skills training were larger than interpersonal skills training (Taylor et al. 2005) • Newly learned skills and changed job behaviour are maintained over time after BMT. Newly learned skills increased over time after BMT likely due to opportunities to practice on the job after more than 1-month post training (Taylor et al. 2005)

(continued)

Table 5.2 (continued)

Designing Training Programmes
• Intrinsic motivation has the largest relative positive impact on training programme evaluation reactions followed by task value and motivation to transfer. However, practitioners are advised to focus on motivation to learn (meta-analytic evidence from Bauer et al. 2016) • Pre-training motivation positively impacted reactions (meta-analytic evidence from Sitzmann et al. 2008) • Reactions to a training programme predict changes in post-training motivation (accounted for an additional 20% of the variance in motivation) over and above pre-training declarative knowledge, pre-training motivation, pre-training self-efficacy. (Meta-analytic evidence from Sitzmann et al. 2008) • Instructor style and human interaction are the strongest predictors of reactions. In courses aimed at changing affective outcomes such as motivation or attitudes e.g. towards diversity, then attention should be paid to programme design features such as instructor and student interaction (Sitzmann et al. 2008) • Reactions influence motivational processes during training as well as their associated outcomes (Sitzmann et al. 2008) • Reactions to a training programme predict changes in post-training motivation (accounted for an additional 20% of the variance in motivation) over and above pre-training declarative (Sitzmann et al. 2008) • Effectiveness of learning, training and development (reaction, learning, behavioural, results) varies with delivery method (e.g., lecture, audio-visual, discussion or multiples), the skill or task being trained (cognitive, interpersonal, and psychomotor) and the criterion used to operationalise effectiveness. Overall the effect sizes are favourable ranging from medium to large indicated that organisational training is generally effective (Arthur et al. 2003) • The largest effect sizes on **reaction** criterion for **cognitive** skills or tasks were from the training methods of self-instruction (mean ds 0.91) (Arthur et al. 2003) • The largest effect sizes on **learning** criterion for **cognitive** skills or tasks were from the training methods of audio-visual and self-instruction (mean ds 1.56), audio-visual and job aid (mean ds 1.49), lecture and audio-visual (mean ds 1.46), lecture, audio-visual and discussion (mean ds 1.35) (Arthur et al. 2003) • The effect sizes on **learning** criterion for **cognitive** and **interpersonal** skills or tasks for lecture and discussion was a mean ds 2.07 (Arthur et al. 2003) • The largest effect sizes on **learning** criterion for **interpersonal** skills or tasks were from the training methods of audio-visual (mean ds 1.44), lecture, audio-visual & teleconference (mean ds 1.29) and lecture (mean ds 0.89) (Arthur et al. 2003)

Designing Training Programmes
• The largest effect sizes on **learning** criterion for **psychomotor** skills or tasks were from the training methods of audio-visual & discussion (mean ds 1.11), lecture, audio-visual (mean ds 0.69) (Arthur et al. 2003) • The largest effect sizes on **behavioural** criterion for **interpersonal** skills or tasks were from the training methods of programmed instruction (mean ds 0.94) followed by audio-visual, programmed instruction and discussion (mean ds 0.75) (Arthur et al. 2003) • The largest effect sizes on **behavioural** criterion for **psychomotor** skills or tasks were from the training methods of equipment simulators (mean *ds* 1.81), audio-visual (mean *ds* 1.45) and lecture (mean *ds* 0.91) (Arthur et al. 2003) • The effect sizes on **results** criterion for **interpersonal** skills or tasks for lecture and discussion was a mean *ds* of 0.79 (Arthur et al. 2003) • Training that includes both cognitive and interpersonal skills or tasks had the largest effects on learning (mean *ds* 2.08) and behavioural criteria (mean *ds* 0.75) followed by psychomotor skills or tasks on learning (mean *ds* 0.80) and behavioural criteria (mean *ds* 0.71). The largest effects on results criteria were from training on interpersonal skills or tasks (mean d 0.88) followed by cognitive skills or tasks (mean *ds* 0.60) and the smallest for psychomotor skills (mean 0.43) (Arthur et al. 2003) • Training reactions should not be used blindly as a surrogate for the assessment of learning of training content. Utility (define) and combined reactions (define) co-relate more strongly with and are therefore better predictors of job performance than affective reactions (define). That is to say that the more behaviourally specific to an act, attitudes are, the more likely they are to predict behaviour (Alliger et al. 1997) • The more specific the content of the attitude measure to the behavioural content or criteria, the higher the relationship between the two. Utility reactions due to their higher level of specify may be more useful for predicting on the job behaviour than affective reactions or measures. Utility reactions also better predicted on-the-job performance than immediate or retained measures of learning (Alliger et al. 1997) • Changes in post-training motivation (accounted for an additional 20% of the variance in motivation) and post-training self-efficacy (accounted for an additional 6% of the variance in self-efficacy) over and above pre-training declarative knowledge, pre-training motivation, pre-training self-efficacy (Sitzmann et al. 2008) • Reactions influence motivational processes during training as well as their associated outcomes. (Meta-analytic evidence from Sitzmann et al. 2008)

(continued)

Table 5.2 (continued)

Designing Training Programmes
• Reactions predict cognitive learning outcomes. Specifically, reactions predicted post-training declarative (accounted for an additional 2% of the variance in post-training declarative knowledge) and procedural knowledge (accounted for an additional 5% of the variance in post-training procedural knowledge (Sitzmann et al. 2008) • Post training self-efficacy is a better predictor of cognitive learning outcomes than are reactions (Sitzmann et al. 2008) • Instructor style and human interaction are strong predictors of reactions but weak predictors of cognitive learning outcomes (Sitzmann et al. 2008) • Reaction measures should not be used as an indicator of learning- if learning measures are difficult to collect- post-training self -efficacy measures could be used as these are a better predictor of post training immediate and delayed procedural knowledge. Thus the information desired from a training programme should determine the choice of evaluation measure (Sitzmann et al. 2008) • The reaction- learning outcomes relationships are stronger when a high level of technology is used to deliver instruction. Specifically, post-training motivation, post-training self-efficacy and post training declarative knowledge scores are larger in programmes with high levels of technology used for instruction. There was no relationship with post training procedural knowledge and the level of technology used. In courses delivered using technology, then attention should be paid to reaction measures (Sitzmann et al. 2008)
Determinants of Training Transfer
Best Available Evidence Findings: • Individual trainee characteristics which are most strongly and consistently predictive of training transfer when source and methods of measurement bias is removed are cognitive ability (.37), conscientiousness (.28) and voluntary participation (.34) • The personality trait neuroticism (.19), pre-training self-efficacy (.22) and motivation (.23) had small to moderate relationships with transfer • Small relationships exist between the personality trait agreeableness (-.03), extraversion (.04) and openness to experience (.08) and training transfer. Small relationships also exist for trainees' age (.04), education (.07), male gender (.12), experience (.09), external locus of control (-.06), job involvement (.04), learning goal orientation (.14), prove-performance goal orientation (.03), avoid-performance goal orientation (-.12) (Source: Blume et al. 2010)

Designing Training Programmes
• The individual trainee characteristics of trainee experience (.06), motivation (.19), pre-training self-efficacy (.23), post-training self-efficacy (.13) were the most strongly and consistently predictive characteristics of transfer of open skills training. Cognitive skills have a greater influence for training transfer of closed skills (.41) than open skills (−.14) (Blume et al. 2010) • Motivation to transfer and expectancy motivation positively impact training transfer. Motivation to transfer is strongest (meta-analytic evidence from Bauer et al. 2016). Motivation to transfer is also an important pathway through which work environment supports (organisational support, supervisor support and peer support) predict training transfer indicating that those designing training should consider factors before, during and after training that affect trainee's motivation to engage and subsequently leverage training content. • Motivation to learn and motivation to transfer positively impact skill acquisition. Motivation to learn is strongest (Bauer et al. 2016) • Environmental context factors which are most strongly and consistently predictive of training transfer when source and methods of measurement bias is removed are transfer climate (.27) and support (.21) (Blume et al. 2010) • Peer support accounts for a slightly higher percentage of training transfer than supervisor or organisational support (Hughes et al. 2019) • Environmental context is more important for training transfer of open skills than closed skills (closed skills are based on training objectives tied to learning specific skills that are to be produced identically in the transfer environment. Open skills are based on training objectives tied to learning principles). (Blume et al. 2010). Leadership training programs that included feedback has a significantly stronger effect size for *transfer* than those with no feedback (t = 5.69) (Lacerenza et al. 2017) • Leadership training programs incorporating information, demonstration and practice-based methods displayed significantly larger effect sizes for *transfer* than programs incorporating only information (t = 4.22) or practice-based methods (t = 7.06). Leadership training programs incorporating all three training methods of information, demonstration and practice displayed significantly larger effect sizes for *transfer* than those incorporating both information and practice-based methods (t = 7.16) or both demonstration and practice-based methods (t = 5.92) (Lacerenza et al. 2017)

(continued)

Table 5.2 (continued)

Designing Training Programmes
• Leadership training programs that included a needs analysis displayed significantly stronger effects for *transfer* (t = 16.14) outcomes than no needs analysis • Leadership training programs that spanned across multiple sessions displayed significantly larger effect sizes than training programs based on one massed sessions, for *transfer* (t = 2.28) (Lacerenza et al. 2017) • Face-to-face leadership training programs displayed significantly stronger effects for *transfer* than virtual programs (t = 5.94) (Lacerenza et al. 2017) • Leadership programs delivered via external instructors displayed significantly stronger effects for *transfer* than those that were self-administered (t = 3.72). There was no difference on *transfer* between programs delivered by internal instructors as compared to self-administered or by external instructors as compared to internal instructors (Lacerenza et al. 2017) • Voluntary leadership programs displayed significantly stronger effects for *transfer* outcomes than involuntary programs (t = 6.26) (Lacerenza et al. 2017) • In leadership training programs, all trained competencies (business, leadership, interpersonal and intrapersonal) were effective. However, some produced significantly greater effects than others. Programs incorporating business competencies displayed greater effects on *transfer* compared to interpersonal, intrapersonal or leadership (Lacerenza et al. 2017) • In designing BMT, transfer of training (effect of training on job behaviour) was largest when at least some of the scenarios that trainees practiced were trainee generated (Taylor et al. 2005) • In designing BMT, training transfer in the form of changes in job behaviour were larger for programmes where trainees set goals, when trainees managers were also trained and when rewards and sanctions were instituted in trainees' workplaces for using/not using newly learned skills (Taylor et al. 2005) • More practice in the form of longer training courses led to greater development of procedural knowledge-skills ($\delta = 0.42$) but had no effect on training transfer in the form of changes in job behaviour (Taylor et al. 2005) • Mixed behaviour modelling training showed greater transfer of training in terms of changes in job behaviour than did positive only training modelling (Taylor et al. 2005). Error management training lead to better ($d = 0.44$) post-training transfer than proceduralised or exploratory (define) training. This demonstrates that deliberately incorporating errors into training can be effective in promoting learning- this in contrast to many traditional training approaches that focus exclusively on correct behaviours and ignore the positives to be gained from making errors during training (Keith and Frese 2008)

Designing Training Programmes
• Error management training did not lead to better within training performance than proceduralised or exploratory training. So while incorporating error training in a training programme slows down within training performance, it does lead to better post training performance. It also highlights to need to measure post training outcome measures more frequently than performance during training (Keith and Frese 2008) • Error management training effectiveness is larger for adaptive ($d = .80$) than analogical ($d = 0.20$) (define) transfer performance. If the goal of training is to transfer learned skills to novel problems that require the development of new solutions, error management training is most useful. If the training goal is to learn and apply just one particular procedure, then training methods that involve direct instruction of this procedure are effective and less time consuming (Keith and Frese 2008) • Active Exploration (define) and Error Encouragement (define) are effective elements of Error management training. The evidence also highlights that exploratory training and practice should be supplemented with error management instructions as these produce significant incremental effects (Keith and Frese 2008) • 3% higher performance (results of Arthur et al. meta-analysis (2003)). In designing BMT, the development of procedural knowledge-skills is enhanced when learning points are used ($\delta = 0.82$) and presented as rule codes ($\delta = 0.78$) (Taylor et al. 2005) • Post-training self-efficacy was 20% higher for trainees receiving instruction via a simulation game than trainees in a comparison (no-training group or group whom received training via another instructional method) group (Sitzmann 2011) • Trainees receiving instruction via a simulation game had 11% higher declarative knowledge ($d = .28$), 14% higher procedural knowledge ($d = .37$) and 9% higher retention levels ($d = .22$) than trainees in the comparison (no-training group or group whom received training via another instructional method) group (Sitzmann 2011) • When the majority of the instruction in the simulation game is active, the simulation game group learned more than the comparison (no-training group or group whom received training via another instructional method) group ($d = .49$). Whereas if the simulation game passively conveys instructional material, the comparison group learn more ($d = -.11$) (Sitzmann 2011)

(continued)

Table 5.2 (continued)

Designing Training Programmes
• When simulation games were used as a supplement to other instructional methods, the simulation game group had higher knowledge levels than the comparison group ($d = .51$) (no-training group or group whom received training via another instructional method). However, when simulation games were used as a standalone instruction, trainees in the comparison group learned more than trainees in the simulation game group ($d = -.12$) (Sitzmann 2011) • The level of organisational support is important for the long-term transfer of training to the workplace and both support from peers and supervisors is more important than organisational support (Hughes et al. 2019) • The motivation of trainees to transfer plays an important role in explaining the ability of supervisory, peer and organisational support to facilitate the long term transfer of training (Hughes et al. 2019) • Employees who are more conscientious are more likely to achieve the maximum transfer of training (Huang et al. 2015)
Training, Job and Organisational Performance
Best Available Evidence Findings:
• Overall, situational characteristics ($\rho = .22$) such as job characteristics, supports and learning opportunities are stronger influencers on engagement in informal learning behaviours than personal characteristics ($\rho = .04$) of individual predispositions and demographics (Cerasoli et al. 2018) • Personality ($\rho = .27$) and learning-related motives ($\rho = .33$) positively impact informal learning behaviours (Cerasoli et al. 2018) • More educated ($\rho = .10$), higher rank ($\rho = .18$), married ($\rho = .17$) employees engage in higher levels of informal learning behaviours. (Cerasoli et al., 2018) • •Job characteristics such as autonomy ($\rho = .31$) and available resources ($\rho = .30$) positively impact informal learning behaviours (Cerasoli et al. 2018) • People support ($\rho = .31$), formal organisational support (e.g. rewards) ($\rho = .38$) and informal organisational support ($\rho = .30$) positively impact informal learning behaviours, most especially formal organisational supports (Cerasoli et al. 2018) • Opportunities for learning are associated with higher levels of informal learning behaviours. (Cerasoli et al. 2018) • Engagement in informal learning behaviours positively impacts general work attitudes ($\rho = .29$) (Cerasoli et al. 2018)

Designing Training Programmes
• Engagement in informal learning is positively associated with knowledge/skill acquisition (ρ = .41) (Cerasoli et al. 2018)
• Engagement in informal learning behaviours is positively associated with performance (ρ = .42) (rated job performance, effectiveness, salary, promotions, project performance), explaining about 18% of the variability in performance. By comparison to meta-analyses on formal training, the results reveal that those whom engage in informal learning behaviours average 32% higher performance than those who do not (Cerasoli et al. 2018)
• Team training (define) positively impacts team functioning (cognitive, affective, process and performance outcomes) (p = 0.34) (Salas et al. 2008)
• Team training positively impacts team level cognitive (p = 0.42), affective (p = 0.35) process (p = 0.44) and performance (p = 0.39) outcomes (Salas et al. 2008)
• Very little difference between task work focused team training interventions (p = 0.35), teamwork focused (p = 0.38) or mixed content focused team training interventions (p = 0.40) for improvement in team performance (Salas et al. 2008)
• For process team outcomes, team task work training (p = 0.28) was not as effective as team working (p = 0.44) or mixed content (p = 0.56) training (Salas et al. 2008)
• Team training worked effectively at improving team performance for teams with both stable (p = 0.54) and ad hoc (p = 0.38) team membership but worked better for stable teams (Salas et al. 2008)
• Team training worked effectively at improving team processes for teams with both stable (p = 0.48) and ad hoc (p = 0.44) team membership but worked better for stable teams (Salas et al. 2008)
• Team training worked effectively at improving team affective outcomes for teams with both stable (p = 0.41) and ad hoc (p = 0.28) team membership but worked better for stable teams (Salas et al. 2008)
• Team coordination training has a moderate positive effect (p = 0.47) on team training outcomes (affective, cognitive, process, performance) (Salas et al. 2008)
• Team cross training has a moderate positive effect (p = 0.44) on team training outcomes (affective, cognitive, process, performance (Salas et al. 2008)
• Training (quantity and quality) positively impacts organisational performance (operational and financial). The strength of the relationship ranges from β = 0.12 to 0.25 (Garavan et al. 2020)

(continued)

Table 5.2 (continued)

Designing Training Programmes
• Training (amount of training, percentage of workers trained, type of training) has a significant positive relationship with organisational performance ($z = 0.09$, $CI = 0.06{:}0.12$) (Tzabbar et al. 2017; Tharenou et al. 2007) • Training impacts financial performance; however, the strength of the relationship is weaker than for organisational performance (Tzabbar et al. 2017; Tharenou et al. 2007) • Organisations benefit from both investments in training which are specific to its processes and activities, in addition to investment in general training which enhances the competencies and skills of employees to perform future roles (Tzabbar et al. 2017; Tharenou et al. 2007) • The impact of training on organisational performance is influenced by the size of the firm, the sector in which it operates, its technological intensity and geographic location (Garavan et al. 2020) • Smaller firms may achieve greater benefits from training than larger firms because they are more likely to conduct in-house and on-the-job training which can be transferred more effectively (Garavan et al. 2020) • Training had a greater impact on employee motivation rather than skill. The impact on motivation was more important for firm performance than was the case for increase in skills (Garavan et al. 2020) • Training has less of an impact on long-term performance rather than short term performance (Garavan et al. 2020) • Training did impact overall financial performance but not ROI or ROE (Garavan et al. 2020) • Depending on the criterion type (effectiveness of training operationalised based on reaction, learning, behavioural and results), the sample-weighted effect size (the effect size for learning was largest 0.63 but the difference in effect size with other criteria was small e.g. reaction 0.60) for organizational training was 0.60–0.63, a medium to large effect. This is an encouraging finding, given the pervasiveness and importance of training to organizations Tzabbar et al. 2017; Tharenou et al. 2007) • Indeed, the magnitude of this effect is comparable to, and in some instances larger than, those reported for other organizational interventions. Specifically, Guzzo et al. (1985) reported a mean effect size of 0.44 for all psychologically based interventions, 0.35 for appraisal and feedback, 0.12 for management by objectives, and 0.75 for goal setting on productivity • Kluger and DeNisi (1996) reported a mean effect size of 0.41 for the relationship between feedback and performance • Neuman et al. (1989) reported a mean effect size of 0.33 between organizational development interventions and attitudes (Arthur et al. 2003)

Does a Training Needs Analysis Enhance the Effectiveness of Training? The answer to this question based on the limited empirical findings and meta-analysis results is a qualified yes. For example, Arthur et al. (2003) in their meta-analysis of the general training literature, did not find significant support for the importance of a training needs analysis. In contrast, Lacerenza et al. (2017) did find support for the role of a training needs analysis in the context of leadership training. The implication of the second meta-analysis finding is that organisations should not adopt a one-size-fits-all approach when it comes to the design of training programmes. In reality, many organisations ignore this important component of the training design process (Garavan et al. 2020).

How Should Organisations Frame the Training in Terms of Attendance Requirements? The review points to conflicting findings concerning voluntary versus mandatory attendance. The results of two meta-analyses provide some guidance on this issue. Bezrukova et al. (2016), in the context of diversity training, found no statistically significant differences in overall effect sizes for mandatory versus voluntary attendance. They did, however, find that there was a larger effect size for behavioural learning outcomes for mandatory versus voluntary participation. Lacerenza et al. (2017) found that voluntary versus mandatory attendance had no impact on individual learning. Voluntary attendance decreased organisational results. They concluded that mandatory attendance policies will foster greater organisational performance outcomes.

How does the Temporal Spacing of Training Sessions and the Length of the Training Impact Effectiveness? There are mixed findings concerning both the spacing of training and the length of training. Lacerenza et al. (2017) for example, found that a distributed approach to training did not result in a significantly greater increase in learning. In the context of the length of training, Bezrukova et al. (2016) found that the duration was positively linked to learning outcomes. Longer training led to more positive attitudes to learning and enhanced diversity knowledge, skills and attitudes. However, often meta-analyses suggest conflicting results. Taylor et al. (2009) for example, did not find support for training length in the context of leadership training.

However, Lacerenza et al. (2017) found that training led to improved organisational and individual learning outcomes.

Are On-Site Programmes More Effective than Off-Site Training Programmes? The findings on this dimension are inconsistent. Bezrukova et al. (2016) found in the context of diversity training that programmes conducted in organisational settings were more effective than these conducted in educational settings. However, they found that participants experienced greater enjoyment of external rather than internal training programmes. Lacerenza et al. (2017) reported evidence that on-site or internal training programmes were more impactful for organisational results compared to external or off-site programmes.

Which Training Methods Are More Effective? A variety of meta-analyses findings speak to this question. For example, Burke and Day (1986) and Taylor et al. (2009) reported findings indicating that practice-based methods are more effective than other delivery methods. Bezrukova et al. (2016) found no significant differences in effect sizes for different types of instruction. However, they found that where diversity training that made use of many instructional methods led to more positive trainee reactions. Lacerenza et al. (2017) found that programmes that utilised multiple methods were significantly more effective than where a single method was used. The use of multiple methods had a major impact on the level of training transfer. A related question concerns the effectiveness of face-to-face versus virtual methods. A number of meta-analyses present different and somewhat conflicting findings. Sitzmann et al. (2006) for example, found that web-based training was more effective than face-to-face training; however, Lacerenza et al. (2017) found in the context of leadership training, that face-to-face was more effective. Howard and Gutworth (2020) investigated different types of virtual reality training and found that virtual reality training programmes, on average, performed better than alternative approaches to developing social skills. Gamified training produced slightly lower levels of learning than programmes that utilised non-immersive displays.

How Relevant is the Training Content in Explaining Training Effectiveness? A number of meta-analyses provide insights on this question. Both Burke and Day (1986) and Taylor et al. (2009) found that learning outcomes were influenced by the content trained. Bezrukova et al. (2016) for example found that training that emphasised awareness type objectives had lower effect sizes compared to attitudinal- and behavioural-focused content. Lacerenza et al. (2017) found that the outcomes were more significant for training that focused on skills. They found that soft-skills training enhanced organisational and individual outcomes compared to hard skills content.

How Important Are Individual Transfer Versus Organisational Transfer Characteristics in Explaining Training Effectiveness? Several meta-analyses provide us with insights on this question. Hughes et al. (2019) for example, found that work environment factors explained unique variance in transfer. Individual characteristics such as motivation to learn, mediated the work environment—transfer link. Peer and supervisor support were particularly important in explaining long-term training transfer. Blume et al. (2010) also found support for the role of work environment supports and that trainee characteristics are shaped by work environment characteristics. Overall, the work environment is particularly important.

Does Training Lead to Firm Performance Outcomes? Four meta-analyses shed light on this question. Tharenou et al. (2007) found a direct link between training and both firm and financial performance of the magnitude .21 and .10, respectively. Lacerenza et al. (2017) found that leadership training enhanced organisational results. Garavan et al. (2020) found that training was positively and directly related to firm performance (.25) but this relationship was influenced by country labour costs and performance orientation. Garavan et al. (2020) found that training was linked to financial performance (.08), however, this was mediated or linked by motivation and human capital. Overall, there is useful evidence that will guide L&D specialists when designing training programmes.

References

Abdullah, M. M. B., Uli, J., & Tarí, J. J. (2008). The influence of soft factors on quality improvement and performance: Perceptions from managers. *Total Quality Management Journal, 20*(5), 436–452.

Aguinis, H., & Kraiger, K. (2009). Benefits of training and development for individuals and teams, organizations, and society. *Annual Review of Psychology, 60*(1), 451–474.

Ahmad, S., & Schroeder, R. G. (2003). The impact of human resource management practices on operational performance: Recognizing country and industry differences. *Journal of Operations Management, 21*(1), 19–43.

Akrofi, S. (2016). Evaluating the effects of executive learning and development on organisational performance: Implications for developing senior manager and executive capabilities. *International Journal of Training and Development, 20*(3), 177–199.

Alliger, G. M., Tannenbaum, S., Bennett, W., Traver, H., & Shotland, A. (1997). A meta-analysis of the relations among training criteria. *Personnel Psychology, 50,* 341–358.

Altinay, L., Altinay, E., & Gannon, J. (2008). Exploring the relationship between the human resource management practices and growth in small service firms. *The Service Industries Journal, 28*(7), 919–937.

Aragon, M. I. B., & Sanz-Valle, R. (2013). Does training managers pay off? *The International Journal of Human Resource Management, 24*(8), 1671–1684.

Aragon, M. I. B., Jiménez-Jiménez, D., & Sanz-Valle, R. (2014). Training and performance: The mediating role of organisational learning. *Business Research Quarterly, 17*(3), 161–173.

Aragon-Sanchez, A., Aragon, M. I. B., & Sanz-Valle, R. (2003). Effect of training on business results. *International Journal of Human Resource Management, 14*(6), 956–980.

Arthur, W., Jr., Bennett, W., Jr., Edens, P. S., & Bell, S. T. (2003). Effectiveness of training in organizations: A meta-analysis of design and evaluation features. *Journal of Applied Psychology, 88*(2), 234–245.

Arunprasad, P. (2017). Inevitable knowledge strategy: A paradigm shift in strategic HRM practices to augment firm's performance. *Employee Relations, 39*(3), 753–774.

Audea, T., Teo, S., & Crawford, J. (2005). HRM professionals and their perceptions of HRM and firm performance in the Philippines. *International Journal of Human Resource Management, 16*(4), 532–552.

Ballot, G., Fakhfakh, F., & Taymaz, E. (2006). Who benefits from training and R&D, the firm or the workers? *British Journal of Industrial Relations, 44*(3), 473–495.

Banerjee, P., Gupta, R., & Bates, R. (2016). Influence of organisational learning culture on knowledge worker's motivation to transfer training: Testing moderating effects of learning transfer climate. *Current Psychology, 36*, 606–617.

Barling, J., Weber, T., & Kelloway, K. (1996). Effects of transformational leadership training on attitudinal and financial outcomes: A Field experiment. *Journal of Applied Psychology, 81*(6), 827–832.

Barrett, A., & O'Connell, P. J. (2001). Does training generally work? The returns to in-company training. *Industrial and Labour Relations Review, 54*(3), 647–662.

Bashir, N., & Long, C. S. (2015). The relationship between training and organisational commitment among academicians in Malaysia. *Journal of Managerial Development, 34*(10), 1227–1245.

Bauer, K. N., Orvis, K. A., Ely, K., & Surface, E. A. (2016). Re-examination of motivation in learning contexts: Meta-analytically investigating the role type of motivation plays in the prediction of key training outcomes. *Journal of Business Psychology, 31*, 33–50.

Beinicke, A., & Bipp, T. (2018). Evaluating training outcomes in corporate eLearning and classroom training. *Vocations and Learning, 11*(3), 501–528.

Bell, J. L., & Grushecky, S. T. (2006). Evaluating the effectiveness of a logger safety training program. *Journal of Safety Research, 37*(1), 53–61.

Berk, A., & Kaše, R. (2010). Establishing the value of flexibility created by training: Applying real options methodology to a single HR practice. *Organization Science, 21*(3), 765–780.

Beugelsdijk, S. (2008). Strategic human resource practices and product innovation. *Organization Studies, 29*, 821–847.

Beynon, H., Grimshaw, D., Rubery, J., & Ward, K. (2002). *Managing employment change: The new realities of work*. Oxford: Oxford University Press.

Bezrukova, K., Spell, C. S., Perry, J. L., & Jehn, K. A. (2016). *A meta-analytical integration of over 40 years of research on diversity training evaluation*. Available from http://scholarship.sha.cornell.edu/articles/974.

Bhatti, W. A., Zaheer, A., & Rehman, K. (2011). The effect of knowledge management practices on organisational performance: A conceptual study. *African Journal of Business Management, 5*, 2847–2853.

Birdi, K. S., Patterson, M. G., & Wood, S. J. (2007). Learning to perform? A comparison of learning practices and organisational performance in profit and non-profit-making sectors in the UK. *International Journal of Training and Development, 11*(4), 265–281.

Birley, S., & Westhead, P. (1990). Private business sales environments in the United Kingdom. *Journal of Business Venturing, 5*(6), 349–373.

Birou, L., Green, K., & Inman, R. (2019). Sustainability knowledge and training: Outcomes and firm performance. *Journal of Manufacturing Technology Management, 30*(2), 294–311.

Black, S., & Lynch, L. (1996). Human-capital investments and productivity. *American Economic Review, 86*(2), 263–267.

Blume, B. D., Ford, J. K., Baldwin, T. T., & Huang, J. L. (2010). Transfer of training: A meta-analytic review. *Journal of Management, 36*(4), 1065–1105.

Boon, M., & van der Eijken, B. (1997). Employee training and productivity in Dutch manufacturing firms. *Statistics Netherlands*, research paper 9716, Voorburg, The Netherlands.

Boselie, P., & Paauwe, J. (2005). Human resource function competencies in European companies. *Personnel Review, 34*(5), 550–566.

Browning, V. (2006). The relationship between HRM practices and service behaviour in South African service organisations. *International Journal of Human Resource Management, 17*(7), 1321–1338.

Buch, R., Dysvik, A., Kuvaas, B., & Nerstad, C. G. (2015). It takes three to tango: Exploring the interplay among training intensity, job autonomy, and supervisor support in predicting knowledge sharing. *Human Resource Management, 54*(4), 623–635.

Buch, R., Kuvaas, B., Dysvik, A., & Schyns, B. (2014). If and when social and economic leader-member exchange relationships predict follower work effort: The moderating role of work motivation. *Leadership and Organisational Development Journal, 35*(8), 725–739.

Burke, M., & Day, R. R. (1986). A cumulative study of the effectiveness of managerial training. *Journal of Applied Psychology, 71*(2), 232–245.

Burton, M. D., & O'Reilly, C. (2004). *Walking the talk: The impact of high commitment values and practices on technology start-ups*. Cornell University, School of Industrial and Labor Relations. Available from http://digitalcommons.ilr.cornell.edu/workingpapers/99.

Cappelli, P., & Neumark, D. (2001). Do "high-performance" work practices improve establishment-level outcomes? *Industrial and Labor Relations Review, 54*(4), 737–775.

Cascio, W. F. (2000). Managing a virtual workplace. *Academy of Management Perspectives, 14,* 81–90.
Cerasoli, C. P., Alliger, G. M., Donsbach, J. S., Mathieu, J. E., Tannenbaum, S. I., & Orvis, K. A. (2018). Antecedents and outcomes of informal learning behaviours: A meta-analysis. *Journal of Business and Psychology, 33*(2), 203–230.
Chatterjee, S., Dandapat, D., & Bagchi, B. (2018). *Efficiency of growth drivers: An analysis of select Indian industries*. New York: Springer.
Chi, N. W., Yu, C. Y., & YunLin, C. Y. (2008). Does training facilitate SME's performance? *International Journal of Human Resource Management, 19*(10), 1962–1975.
Chinomona, R. (2013). Business owner's expertise, employee skills training and business performance: A small business perspective. *Journal of Applied Business Research, 29*(6), 1883–1896.
Cho, T., & Yoon, S. (2009). Human resource management, individualism-collectivism, and individual performance among public employees: A test of the main and moderating effects. *The Korean Journal of Policy Studies, 23*(2), 57–87.
Cho, Y., & Egan, T. M. (2009). Action learning research: A systematic review and conceptual framework. *Human Resource Development Review, 8*(4), 431–462.
Chowhan, J. (2016). Unpacking the black box: Understanding the relationship between strategy, HRM practices, innovation and organizational performance. *Human Resource Management Journal, 26*(2), 112–133.
CIPD. (2017). *To gig or not to gig? Stories from the modern economy*. Survey Report. Available from https://www.cipd.co.uk/Images/to-gig-or-not-to-gig_2017-stories-from-the-modern-economy_tcm18-18955.pdf.
Cjoi, Y., & Dickson, D. R. (2009). A case study into the benefits of management training programs: Impacts on hotel employee turnover and satisfaction level. *Journal of Human Resources in Hospitality & Tourism, 9*(1), 103–116.
Cobblah, M. C., & Van der Walt, T. B. (2016). Staff training and development programmes and work performance in the university libraries in Ghana. *Information Development, 33*(4), 375–392.
Coetzee, R., Visagie, J., & Ukpere, W. I. (2014). Responding to change in a large organisation from a leadership angle. *Mediterranean Journal of Social Sciences, 5*(20), 827.

Colquitt, J. A., LePine, J. A., & Noe, R. A. (2000). Toward an integrative theory of training motivation: A meta-analytic path analysis of 20 years of research. *Journal of Applied Psychology, 85*(5), 678–707.

Cooke, N. J., Gorman, J. C., Duran, J. L., & Taylor, A. R. (2007). Team cognition in experienced command-and-control teams. *Journal of Experimental Psychology: Applied, 13,* 146–157.

D'Arcimoles, C. (1997). Human resource policies and company performance: A quantitative approach using longitudinal data. *Organizational Studies, 18,* 857–874.

Darwish, T. K., Singh, S., & Mohamed, A. F. (2013). The role of strategic HR practices in organisational effectiveness: An empirical investigation in the country of Jordan. *International Journal of Human Resource Management, 24*(17), 3343–3362.

Delaney, T. J., & Huselids, M. A. (1996). The impact of human resource practices on perceptions of organisational performance. *Academy of Management Journal, 39*(4), 949–969.

Deng, J., Menguc, B., & Benson, J. (2003). The impact of human resource management on export performance of Chinese manufacturing enterprises. *Thunderbird International Business Review, 45*(4), 409–420.

Dermol, V., & Cater, T. (2013). The influence of training and training transfer factors on organisational learning and performance. *Personnel Review, 42*(3), 324–348.

Dhar, R. L. (2015). Service quality and the training of employees: The mediating role of organizational commitment. *Tourism Management, 46,* 419–430.

Diaz-Fernandez, M., Bornay-Barrachina, M., & Lopez-Cabrales, A. (2015). Innovation and firm performance: The role of human resource management practices. *Evidence-Based HRM, 3*(1), 64–80.

Donovan, J. J., & Radosevich, D. J. (1999). A meta-analytic review of the distribution of practice effect: Now you see it, now you don't. *Journal of Applied Psychology, 84*(5), 795–805.

Dostie, B. (2018). The impact of training on innovation. *ILR Review, 71*(1), 64–87.

Dysvik, A., & Kuvaas, B. (2008). The relationship between perceived training opportunities, work motivation and employee outcomes. *International Journal of Training and Development, 12*(3), 138–157.

Ellinger, A. D., Ellinger, A. E., & Keller, S. B. (2003). Supervisory coaching behavior, employee satisfaction, and warehouse employee performance: A dyadic perspective in the distribution industry. *Human Resource Development Quarterly, 14*(4), 435–458.

Ellis, A. P. J., Bell, B. S., Ployhart, R. E., Hollenbeck, J. R., & Ilgen, D. R. (2005). An evaluation of generic teamwork skills training and action teams: Effects on cognitive and skills-based outcomes. *Personnel Psychology, 58,* 641–672.

Ely, R. (2004). A field study of group diversity, participation in diversity education programs, and performance. *Journal of Organizational Behaviour, 25,* 755–780.

Esteban-Lloret, N. N., Aragon-Sanchez, A., & Carrasco, A. (2016). Determinants of employee training: Impact on organisational legitimacy and organisational performance. *International Journal of Human Resource Management, 29*(6), 1–22.

Feng, T., Wang, D., & Prajogo, D. (2014). Incorporating human resource management initiatives into customer services: Empirical evidence from Chinese manufacturing firms. *Industrial Marketing Management, 43,* 126–135.

Fletcher, L., Alfes, K., & Robinson, D. (2016). The relationship between perceived training and development and employee retention: The mediating role of work attitudes. *International Journal of Human Resource Management, 29*(18), 2701–2728.

Frenkel, S. J., & Bednall, T. (2016). How training and promotion opportunities, career expectations, and two dimensions of organizational justice explain discretionary work effort. *Human Performance, 29*(1), 16–32.

Gainey, T. W., & Klass, B. S. (2003). The outsourcing of training and development: Factors impacting client satisfaction. *Journal of Management, 29*(2), 207–229.

Garavan, T., McCarthy, A., Lai, Y., Murphy, K., Sheehan, M., & Carbery, R. (2020). Training and organisational performance: A meta-analysis of temporal, institutional, and organisational context moderators. *Human Resource Management Journal,* in-press.

García-Bernal, J., Gargallo-Castel, A., Marzo-Navarro, M., & Rivera-Torres, P. (2005). Job satisfaction: Empirical evidence of gender differences. *Women in Management Review, 20*(4), 279–288.

Gavino, M. C., Wayne, S. J., & Erdogan, B. (2012). Discretionary and transactional human resource practices and employee outcomes: The role of perceived organizational support. *Human Resource Management, 51*(5), 665–686.

Gelade, G. A., & Ivery, M. (2003). The impact of human resource management and work climate on organizational performance. *Personnel Psychology, 56*, 383–404.

Georgellis, Y., Lange, T., & Tabbuma, V. (2012). The impact of life events on job satisfaction. *Journal of Vocational Behaviour, 80*(2), 464–473.

Giangreco, M. F., Suter, J. C., & Doyle, M. B. (2010). Paraprofessionals in inclusive schools: A review of recent research. *Journal of Educational and Psychological Consultation, 20*(1), 41–57.

Glaub, M. E., Frese, M., Fischer, S., & Hoppe, M. (2014). Increasing personal initiative in small business managers or owners leads to entrepreneurial success: A theory-based controlled randomized field intervention for evidence-based management. *Academy of Management Learning & Education, 13*(3), 354–379.

Glaveli, N., & Karassavidou, E. (2011). Exploring a possible route through which training affects organizational performance: The case of a Greek bank. *The International Journal of Human Resource Management, 22*(14), 2892–2923.

Gooderham, P., Ringdal, K., & Parry, E. (2006). *The impact of human resource management practices on the performance of European firms*. Copenhagen Business School Conference on HRM and Knowledge-Related Performance.

Gould-Williams, J. (2007). HR practices, organizational climate and employee outcomes: Evaluating social exchange relationships in local government. *The International Journal of Human Resource Management, 18*(9), 1627–1647.

Grossman, R., & Salas, E. (2011). The transfer of training: What really matters? *International Journal of Training and Development, 15*(2), 103–120.

Guan, X., & Frenkel, S. (2018). How HR practice, work engagement and job crafting influence employee performance. *Chinese Management Studies, 12*, 591–607.

Gupta-Potnuru, R. M., & Sahoo, C. K. (2016). HRD interventions, employee competencies and organizational effectiveness: An empirical study. *European Journal of Training and Development, 40*(5), 345–365.

Gurbuz, S., & Mert, I. S. (2011). Impact of the strategic human resource management on organizational performance: Evidence from Turkey. *The International Journal of Human Resource Management, 22*(8), 1803–1822.

Gutiérrez-Gutiérrez, L. J., Bustinza, O. F., & Barrales-Moline, V. (2012). Six sigma, absorptive capacity and organisational learning orientation. *International Journal of Production Research, 50*(3), 661–675.

Guzzo, R. A., Jette, R. D., & Katzell, R. A. (1985). The effects of psychologically based intervention programs on worker productivity: A meta-analysis. *Personnel Psychology, 38*(2), 275–291.

Harel, G. H., & Tzafrir, S. S. (1999). The effect of human resource management practices on the perceptions of organizational and market performance of the firm. *Human Resource Management, 38*(3), 185–199.

Hassan, M. G., Hassan, S., Khan, M. F. A., & Iqbal, A. (2013). Impact of HR practices on employee satisfaction and employee loyalty: An empirical study of government owned public sector banks of Pakistan. *Middle East Journal of Scientific Research, 16*(1), 1–8.

Heyler, R., & Lee, D. (2014). The role of work experience in the future employability of higher education graduates. *Higher Education Quarterly, 68*(3), 348–372.

Holton, E. F., Bates, R. A., & Ruona, W. E. A. (2000). Development of a generalised learning transfer inventory. *Human Resource Development Quarterly, 11*(4), 333–360.

Holzer, H. J., Block, R., Cheatman, M., & Knott, J. H. (1993). Are training subsidies for firms effective? The Michigan experience. *Industrial and Labour Relations Review, 46*(4), 625–636.

Horgan, J., & Muhlau, P. (2006). Human resource systems and employee performance in Ireland and the Netherlands: A test of the complementarity hypothesis. *International Journal of Human Resource Management, 17*(3), 414–439.

Howard, M. C., & Gutworth, M. B. (2020). A meta-analysis of virtual reality training programs for social skill development. *Computers and Education, 144*, 1–19.

Howardson, G. N., & Behrend, T. S. (2016). Coming full circle with reactions: Understanding the structure and correlates of trainee reactions through the affect circumplex. *Academy of Management Learning & Education, 15*(3), 471–492.

Huang, J. L., Blume, B. D., Ford, J. K., & Baldwin, T. T. (2015). A tale of two transfers: Disentangling maximum and typical transfer and their respective predictors. *Journal of Business Psychology, 30,* 709–732.

Huang, J. L., Ford, J. K., & Ryan, A. M. (2017). Ignored no more: Within-person variability enables better understanding of training transfer. *Personal Psychology, 70,* 557–596.

Hughes, A., Zajac, S., Woods, A. L., & Salas, E. (2019). The role of work environment in training sustainment: A meta-analysis. *Human Factors, 62*(1), 1–18.

Hurtz, G. M., & Williams, K. J. (2009). Attitudinal and motivational antecedents of participation in voluntary employee development activities. *Journal of Applied Psychology, 94*(3), 635–653.

Jiang, J., Wang, S., & Zhao, S. (2012). Does HRM facilitate employee creativity and organizational innovation? A study of Chinese firms. *International Journal of Human Resource Management, 23*(19), 4025–4047.

Jimenez-Jimenez, D., & Sanz-Valle, R. (2005). Innovation and human resource management fit: An empirical study. *International Journal of Manpower, 26*(4), 364–381.

Jung, Y., & Takeuchi, N. (2019). Testing mediation effects of social and economic exchange in linking organizational training investment to employee outcomes. *Personnel Review, 48*(2), 306–323.

Kaminski, M. (2001). Unintended consequences: Organisational practices and their impact on workplace safety and productivity. *Journal of Occupational Health Psychology, 6*(2), 127–138.

Kampkotter, P., & Marggraf, K. (2015). Do employees reciprocate to intra-firm trainings? An analysis of absenteeism and turnover rates. *International Journal of Human Resource Management, 26*(22), 2888–2907.

Karami, A., Jones, B. M., & Kakabadse, N. K. (2008). Does strategic human resource management matter in high-tech sector? Some learning points for SME managers. *Corporate Governance International Journal of Business in Society, 8*(1), 7–17.

Katou, A. A., Budhwar, P. S., & Patel, C. (2014). Content vs. process in the HRM- performance relationship: An empirical examination. *Human Resource Management 53,* 527–544.

Keith, N., & Frese, M. (2008). Effectiveness of error management training: A meta-analysis. *Journal of Applied Psychology, 93,* 59–69.

Kim, Y., & Ployhart, R. E. (2014). The effects of staffing and training on firm productivity and profit growth before, during and after the Great Recession. *Journal of Applied Psychology, 99*(3), 361–389.

Kirkpatrick, D. L. (1987). Evaluation of training. In R. L. Craig (Ed.), *Training and development handbook: A guide to human resource development* (pp. 301–319). New York: McGraw-Hill.

Kitching, J., & Blackburn, R. A. (2002). *The nature of training and motivation to train in small firms*. Small Business Research Centre, Kingston University. Available from http://dera.ioe.ac.uk/4691/1/RR330.pdf.

Kluger, A. N., & DeNisi, A. (1996). The effects of feedback interventions on performance: A historical review, a meta-analysis, and a preliminary feedback intervention theory. *Psychological Bulletin, 119*(2), 254–284.

Koch, M. J., & McGrath, R. G. (1996). Improving labour productivity: Human resource management policies do matter. *Strategic Management Journal, 17*(5), 335–354.

Kodwani, A. (2017). Decoding training effectiveness: The role of organisational factors. *Journal of Workplace Learning, 29*(3), 200–216.

Kodwani, A. D., & Prashar, S. (2019). Exploring the influence of pre-training factors on training effectiveness-moderating role of trainees' reaction: A study in the public sector in India. *Human Resource Development International, 22*(3), 283–304.

Kooij, D., Guest, D., Clinton, M., Knight, T., Jansen, P., & Dikkers, J. (2013). How the impact of HR practices on employee well-being and performance changes with age? *Human Resource Management Journal, 23*(1), 18–35.

Kown, K., & Rupp, D. E. (2013). High-performer turnover and firm performance: The moderating role of human capital investment and firm reputation. *Journal of Organisational Behaviour, 34*(1), 129–150.

Kraiger, K., & Ford, J. K. (2007). The expanding role of workplace training: Themes and trends influencing training research and practice. In L. L. Koppes (Ed.), *Historical perspectives in industrial and organizational psychology* (pp. 281–309). Mahwah, NJ: Lawrence Erlbaum Associates Publishers.

Kraiger, K., Ford, J. K., & Salas, E. (1993). Application of cognitive, skill-based and affective theories of learning outcomes to new methods of training evaluation. *Journal of Applied Psychology, 78*, 311–328.

Kulik, C. C., & Kulik, J. A. (1991). Effectiveness of computer-based instruction: An updated analysis. *Computers in Human Behaviour, 7*, 75–94.

Kumar, S., & Liu, D. (2005). Impact of globalisation on entrepreneurial enterprises in the world markets. *International Journal of Management and Enterprise Development, 2*(1), 46–64.

Lacerenza, C. N., Reyes, D. L., Marlow, S. L., Joseph, D. L., & Salas, E. (2017). Leadership training design, delivery, and implementation: A meta-analysis. *Journal of Applied Psychology, 102*(12), 1686–1718.

Lam, T., Lo, A., & Chan, J. (2002). New employees' turnover intentions and organizational commitment in the Hong Kong hotel industry. *Journal of Hospitality & Tourism Research, 26*(3), 217–234.

Lau, C. M., & Ngo, H. Y. (2004). The HR system, organisational culture, and product innovation. *International Business Review, 13*(6), 685–703.

Laursen, K., & Foss, N. (2003). New human resource management practices, complementarities and the impact on innovation performance. *Cambridge Journal of Economics, 27*(2), 243–263.

LeBlanc, G., & Nguyen, N. (1996). Cues used by customers evaluating corporate image in service firms: An empirical study in financial institutions. *International Journal of Service Industry Management, 7*(2), 44–56.

Liao, H., & Chuang, A. (2004). A multilevel investigation of factors influencing employee service performance and customer outcomes. *The Academy of Management Journal, 47*(1), 41–58.

Litz, R. A., & Stewart, A. C. (2000). Trade-name franchise membership as a human resource management strategy: Does buying group training deliver 'true value' for small retailers? *Entrepreneurship Theory and Practice, 25*(1), 125–135.

Liu, M. T., Wong, I. A., Shi, G., Chu, R., & Brock, J. L. (2014). The impact of corporate social responsibility (CSR) performance and perceived brand quality on customer-based brand preference. *Journal of Services Marketing, 28*(3), 181–194.

Liu, N. C., & Liu, M. S. (2011). Human resource practices and individual knowledge-sharing behaviour—An empirical study for Taiwanese R&D professionals. *The International Journal of Human Resource Management, 22*(4), 981–997.

Lowell, V. L., & Morris, J. (2019). Leading changes to professional training in the multigenerational office: Generational attitudes and preferences towards learning and technology. *Performance Improvement Quarterly, 32*(2), 111–135.

Lux, M., Strohmaier, M., Dösinger, G., & Tochtermann, K. (2007). The web 2.0 way of learning with technologies. *International Journal of Learning Technology, 3*(1), 87–107.

McNamara, T. K., Parry, E., Lee, J., & Pitt-Catsouphes, M. (2011). The effect of training on organisational performance: Differences by age composition and cultural context. *The International Journal of Human Resource Management, 23*(6), 1226–1244.

Meschi, P., & Metais, E. (1998). A socio-economic study of companies through their training policies: New empirical considerations in the French context. *MIR: Management International Review, 38*(1), 25–48.

Miller, D., & Lee, J. (2001). The people make the process: Commitment to employees, decision making, and performance. *Journal of Management, 27*(2), 163–189.

Murray, B., & Raffaele, G. C. (1997). Single-site, results-level evaluation of quality awareness training. *Human Resource Development Quarterly, 8*(3), 229–245.

Nasurdin, A. M., Ahmad, N. H., & Tan, C. L. (2014). Cultivating service-oriented citizenship behavior among hotel employees: The instrumental roles of training and compensation. *Service Business*. https://doi.org/10.1007/s11628-014-0230-5.

Neuman, G. A., Edwards, J. E., & Raju, N. S. (1989). Organizational development interventions: A meta-analysis of their effects on satisfaction and other attitudes. *Personnel Psychology, 42*(3), 461–489.

Odle-Dusseau, H. N., Hammer, L. B., Crain, T., & Bodner, T. E. (2015). The influence of family-supportive supervisor training on employee job performance and attitudes: An organizational work-family intervention. *Journal of Occupational Health Psychology, 21*(3), 296–308.

Okay-Somerville, B., & Scholarios, D. (2019). A multilevel examination of skills-oriented human resource management and perceived skill utilization during recession: Implications for the well-being of all workers. *Human Resource Management, 58*(2), 139–154.

Otoo, F. (2019). Human resource development (HRD) practices and banking industry effectiveness: The mediating role of employee competencies. *European Journal of Training and Development, 43*(3/4), 250–271.

Park, Y., & Jacobs, R. L. (2011). The influence of investment in workplace learning on learning outcomes and organisational performance. *Human Resource Development Quarterly, 22*(4), 437–458.

Peccei, R., & Rosenthal, R. (2001). Delivering customer-oriented behaviour through empowerment: An empirical test of HRM assumptions. *Journal of Management Studies, 38*(6), 831–857.

Piaralal, N. K., Mat, N., Piaralal, S. K., & Bhatti, M. A. (2014). Human resource management factors and service recovery performance in Malaysian life insurance industry. *European Journal of Training and Development, 38*(6), 524–552.

Pratono, A. H., & Mahmood, R. (2016). Entrepreneurial orientation and firm performance: How can small and medium-sized enterprises survive environmental turbulence? *Pacific Science Review: Humanities and Social Sciences, 1*(2), 85–91.

Quratulain, S., Khan, A. K., Sabharwal, M., & Javed, B. (2019). Effect of self-efficacy and instrumentality beliefs on training implementation behaviours: Testing the moderating effect of organisational climate. *Review of Public Personnel Administration*, in-press.

Raineri, A. (2017). Linking human resources practices with performance: The simultaneous mediation of collective affective commitment and human capital. *The International Journal of Human Resource Management, 28*(22), 3149–3178.

Riley, S. M., Michael, S. C., & Mahoney, J. T. (2017). Human capital matters: Market valuation of firm investments in training and the role of complementary assets. *Strategic Management Journal, 38*(9), 1895–1914.

Sahoo, M., & Mishra, S. (2019). Effects of trainee characteristics, training attitudes and training need analysis on motivation to transfer training. *Management Research Review, 42*(2), 215–238.

Salas, E., Diaz-Granados, D., Klein, C., Burke, S., & Stagl, K. C. (2008). Does team training improve team performance? *Human Factors, 50*(6), 903–933.

Salas, E., Weaver, S. J., & Shuffler, M. L. (2012). Learning, training, and development in organizations. In S. W. J. Kozlowski (Ed.), *Oxford library of psychology. The Oxford handbook of organizational psychology, Vol. 1* (pp. 330–372). Oxford: Oxford University Press.

Santos, J. P., Caetano, A., & Tavares, S. M. (2015). Is training leaders in functional leadership a useful tool for improving the performance of leadership functions and team effectiveness? *The Leadership Quarterly, 26*(3), 470–484.

Shaw, J. D., Delery, J. E., Jenkins, G. D., & Gupta, N. (1998). An organizational-level analysis of voluntary and involuntary turnover. *Academy of Management Journal, 41,* 511–525.

Shen, J., & Tang, C. (2018). How does training improve customer service quality? The roles of transfer of training and job satisfaction. *European Management Journal, 36*(6), 708–716.

Sitzmann, T. (2011). A meta-analytic examination of the instructional effectiveness of computer-based simulation games. *Personnel Psychology, 64,* 489–528.

Sitzmann, T., & Weinhardt, J. M. (2015). Training engagement theory: A multilevel perspective on the effectiveness of work-related training. *Journal of Management, 44*(2), 732–756.

Sitzmann, T., Brown, K. G., Casper, W. J., & Ely, K. (2008). A review and meta-analysis of the nomological network of trainee reactions. *Journal of Applied Psychology, 93*(2), 280–295.

Sitzmann, T., Kraiger, K., Stewart, D., & Wisher, R. (2006). The comparative effectiveness of web-based and classroom instruction: A meta-analysis. *Personnel Psychology, 59*(3), 623–664.

Stone, D. L., & Deadrick, D. L. (2015). Challenges and opportunities affecting the future of human resource management. *Human Resource Management Review, 25*(2), 139–145.

Sung, S. Y., & Choi, J. N. (2012). Effects of team knowledge management on the creativity and financial performance of organisational teams. *Organisational Behaviour and Human Decision Processes, 118*(1), 4–13.

Sung, S. Y., & Choi, J. N. (2014). Do organizations spend wisely on employees? Effects of training and development investments on learning and innovation in organizations. *Journal of Organisational Behaviour, 35*, 393–412.

Tan, J., Hall, R. J., & Boyce, C. (2003). The role of employee reactions in predicting training effectiveness. *Human Resource Development Quarterly, 14*(4), 397–411.

Taylor, P. J., Russ-Eft, D. F., & Chan, D. W. L. (2005). A meta-analytic review of behaviour modelling training. *Journal of Applied Psychology, 90*(4), 692–709.

Taylor, P. J., Russ-Eft, D. F., & Taylor, H. (2009). Transfer of management training from alternative perspectives. *Journal of Applied Psychology, 94*, 104–121.

Tessema, M. T., & Soeters, J. (2006). Challenges and prospects of HRM in developing countries: Testing the HRM-performance link in the Eritean civil service. *International Journal of Human Resource Management, 17*, 105–186.

Tharenou, P., Saks, A. M., & Moore, C. (2007). A review of critique of research on training and organisational-level outcomes. *Human Resource Management Review, 17*, 251–273.

Tracey, J. B., Tannenbaum, S. I., & Kavanaugh, M. J. (1995). Applying trained skills on the job: The importance of the work environment. *Journal of Applied Psychology, 80*, 239–252.

Tremblay, M., Cloutier, J., Simard, G., Chenevert, D., & Vandenberghe, C. (2010). The role of HRM practices, procedural justice, organizational support and trust in organizational commitment and in-role and extra-role performance. *The International Journal of Human Resource Management, 21*(3), 405–433.

Tzabbar, D., Tzafrir, S., & Baruch, Y. (2017). A bridge over troubled water: Replication, integration and extension of the relationship between HRM practices and organisational performance using moderating meta-analysis. *Human Resource Management Review, 27*(1), 134–148.

Tzafrir, S. (2005). The relationship between trust, HRM practices and firm performance. *International Journal of Human Resource Management, 16*(9), 1600–1622.

Úbeda-García, M. (2005). Training and business performance: The Spanish case. *The International Journal of Human Resource Management, 16*(9), 1691–1710.

Ubeda-Garcia, M., Marco, B., Sabater, V., & Garcia-Lillo, F. (2013). Training policy and organisational performance in the Spanish hotel industry. *International Journal of Human Resource Management, 24*(15), 2851–2875.

Unger, J. M., Rauch, A., Frese, M., & Rosenbusch, N. (2011). Human capital and entrepreneurial success: A meta-analytical review. *Journal of Business Venturing, 26*(3), 341–358.

Wickramasinghe, V., & Liyanage, S. (2013). Effects of high performance work practices on job performance in project-based organizations. *Project Management Journal, 44*(3), 64–77.

Wright, P. M., Dunford, B. B., & Snell, S. A. (2001). Human resources and the resource-based view of the firm. *Journal of Management, 27*(6), 701–721.

Yang, B., Watkins, K. E., & Marsick, V. J. (2004). The construct of the learning organization: Dimensions, measurement, and validation. *Human Resource Development Quarterly, 15*(1), 31–55.

Yang, T., Xun, J., & He, X. (2015). British SMEs' e-commerce technological investments and firm performance: An RBV perspective. *Technology Analysis & Strategic Management, 27*(5), 586–603.

Zhang, D. (2004). Virtual mentor and the lab system: Toward building an interactive, personalized, and in an intelligent eLearning environment. *Journal of Computer Information Systems, 44*, 35–43.

6

Suggestions for Research and Practice

Abstract This chapter summarises the research on the effectiveness of learning and development in organisations. It makes research recommendations of the content of effectiveness research, recommendations for research design, and recommendations for practice. It summarises key gaps in the research base, as well as highlighting practice recommendations that learning and development specialists can implement to enhance the overall effectiveness of these activities in contributing to organisational performance.

Keywords Gaps in research on effectiveness · Key content areas for future research · Key methodological challenges · Implications for practice

6.1 Introduction

The previous section suggested that although a lot of research has investigated training effectiveness in organisations, there is very limited research that links together the various elements of our conceptual model. Therefore, in this final chapter we focus on two important issues:

T. N. Garavan et al.
Learning and Development Effectiveness in Organisations,
https://doi.org/10.1007/978-3-030-48900-7_6

the content issues that researchers should focus on, and recommendations for research designs. We then address a number of practice issues for L&D practitioners and other stakeholders within the organisation.

6.2 Recommendations on the Content of Empirical Training Effectiveness Research

Regarding the content of empirical training effectiveness research, we have some suggestions for future research. Table 6.1 summarises the research issues that arise in respect of each component of the model. As we highlighted in the previous section, not all aspects of the training effectiveness process are getting scholarly attention. We suggest that there is a need for training scholars to invest more of their effort in understanding how training works and how effectively it works from the perspective of multiple organisational actors. In this section we prioritise three pressing issues.

6.2.1 Linking Individual-Level Learning Outcomes to Organisational Performance

A significant 'black box' issue within the current literature concerns the linkage of individuals KSAs to organisational performance. Ployhart et al. (2014) in a seminal contribution argued that organisational performance has its origins in individual KSAs. Ployhart and Moliterno (2011) defined organisational human capital as a 'unit level resource that is created from the emergence of individual KSAs' and they proposed an emergence model to conceptualise this emergence to the organisation level. Other more recent contributions have also engaged with the link between individual human capital and organisational performance, such as Wright and McMahon (2011). Researchers in the training field have largely focused on the training practices that are used to develop human capital but ignored the human capital component. Thus, conceptualisations of human capital, where they are explicitly mentioned, are

Table 6.1 Key findings and research implications arising from each component of the model

Specific Model Component	Key Findings and Research Questions
Environmental/ Organisational Inputs	**Key Findings:** • Important environmental inputs provide triggers for organisations to conduct training • Organisational inputs such as strategy, culture and climate for learning impact the effectiveness of training through their influence on training participation and engagement and fit between the training and strategy/culture/climate • There are major gaps and unresolved issues when it comes to their influence on training. Insufficient attention given to workforce diversity, changing job and skills, technology and knowledge intensity and characteristics of the L&D function • What happens prior to training has a major impact on training effectiveness. Contextual factors such as the clarity of the organisation's business and HR strategy, the availability of rewards and sanctions and the nature of work processes impact employee motivation for training, their engagement and willingness to participate and the types of goals they set for training **Future Research Questions** • Researchers need to increase their understanding of the inputs that shape training. This should focus in particular on macro-level environmental factors • The particular roles of organisational strategy, HR strategy and L&D strategy need particular attention. There is a lack of a critical mass of research studies • There is currently poor reporting of context in studies on training effectiveness. Therefore, researchers need to pay attention to describing multiple levels of context, in particular, the national institutional and cultural context, industry, type of firm, organisation strategy and culture and L&D strategy and the key triggers for training • Insufficient attention has been given to the study of training in the context of other L&D and HR practices. We need more insights into how other L&D and HR practices impact training effectiveness • There are significant unresolved issues concerning whether the level of technology intensity, sector and organisation size are important in explaining training effectiveness

(continued)

Table 6.1 (continued)

Specific Model Component	Key Findings and Research Questions
	• Researchers need to more fully understand how characteristics of the L&D function, including its maturity, its use of technology, the size of the function, the expertise base of the L&D function and its use of sub-contracting and external versus internal training expertise impact training effectiveness
Individual Trainee Inputs	**Key Findings:** • The cognitive abilities and level of knowledge of the trainee are important predictors of learning outcomes • Motivational characteristics, values towards learning, personality traits such as conscientiousness and instrumentality are important in explaining learning outcomes and training effectiveness • Trainability which is concerned with a trainee's capacity to learn the job, is highlighted as particularly important in explaining the mastery of skills • Trainee characteristics explain learning outcomes in both face-to-face and virtual training including e-learning, simulations and in-tray exercises • Trainee characteristics interact with factors such as perceptions of support, organisational policies, rewards/sanctions to predict participation in training, learning outcomes and training effectiveness **Future Research Questions** • Researchers should conduct research on the role of individual characteristics in the context of remote learning contexts, virtual learning and learning in different cultural contexts • Insufficient research to date has investigated the impact of trainee characteristics on learning outcomes and training effectiveness over time • How do trainee individual differences account for learning outcomes and training effectiveness in blended learning situations? • What role do individual differences play in self-directed and voluntary training situations compared to mandated training?

(continued)

Table 6.1 (continued)

Specific Model Component	Key Findings and Research Questions
	• Researches need to more fully understand how individual differences interact with the trainee level within the organisation and other characteristics such as type of employment contract, working hours, job and organisational tenure
Training Design Inputs	**Key Findings:** • The quality of the needs analysis process is important in providing the trainee and trainer with important knowledge on learning objectives and ultimately training effectiveness • Mixed findings on whether mandatory or voluntary attendance policy is more important for trainee motivation to participate, trainee engagement, reactions and learning outcomes • Researchers have investigated a broad range of training design characteristics but primarily in face-to-face classroom training situations • The effectiveness of particular training design features is contingent on the knowledge or skills to be trained and the expected learning outcomes • Training that is effectively designed to build in more self-directed features, self-regulated learning processes and active practice into the instruction process will be more effective in terms of learning outcomes and overall training effectiveness • There are many unanswered questions concerning the effectiveness of technology-based training for soft-skills development **Future Research Questions** • Researchers need to more fully understand which types of learning needs will be more effectively addressed using instructor-led training versus e-learning, remote learning or blended learning • We lack strong research insights concerning team training interventions, blended learning and 1:1 training in enhancing training effectiveness • Researchers need to significantly understand the importance of trainer characteristics for training effectiveness. Specific knowledge gaps exist with respect to internal versus external trainers and the impacts of the customisation of training • How effective are social networks, MOOCs, OCOP forums in terms of learning outcomes and overall training effectiveness?

(continued)

Table 6.1 (continued)

Specific Model Component	Key Findings and Research Questions
Learner Reactions to Training	**Key Findings:** • Trainee or learner reactions are generally effective predictors of perceived and objective learning outcomes • Satisfaction with training is influenced by both cognitive and affective reactions to training **Future Research Questions** • What influence to features of training design such as duration, team location and spacing of training have on trainee reactions? • There is a need for increased research on how reactions to training change over time and their impact on learning • We need more insights concerning who training participants with multiple roles report reactions to training (participant and manager of other participants) • Researchers need to more fully understand the impact of different training delivery formats in reactions of trainees • How do trainee reactions interact with motivation to learn, instrumentality and self-efficacy for learning?
Organisational Reactions to Training	**Key Findings:** • There is a theory suggesting that a variety of organisational processes will influence organisational reactions but research is non-existent **Future Research Questions** • How does the quality of particular training programmes impact organisational actors' perceptions of training generally? • What is the impact of positive/negative reactions to training on future resource allocation for training? • What are the factors that influence course recommendations intentions and how do these recommendations impact resource allocation and the profile of training within the organisation? • What factors shape the reactions of non-participants such as first-line supervisors and managers to (nominating) to training programmes?

(continued)

Table 6.1 (continued)

Specific Model Component	Key Findings and Research Questions
Individual Learning Outcomes	**Key Findings:** • There is a generally positive relationship between positive reactions and learning outcomes; however, it is unclear as to whether positive reactions are essential for learning • The link between trainee reactions and learning outcomes will likely vary by the nature of the reactions (affective vs. cognitive vs. satisfaction) **Future Research Questions** • How does the strength of the relationship between trainee reactions and learning vary over time? • How do different trainee characteristics interact with reactions to influence learning outcomes? • Do learner characteristics such as motivation to learn, self-efficacy, instrumentality and personality characteristics influence the level of earning that occurs in different training formats?
Organisational Learning Outcomes	**Key Findings:** • Theoretical suggestions but terra incognita when it comes to research findings **Future Research Questions** • How do socialisation/indoctrination processes related to learning outcomes of training influence the importance attached to training within the organisation? • How do organisations use feedback from training courses to develop insights about new and continued KSAs in organisations? • How does the success or failure of specific training programmes inform future knowledge and learning about selecting and preparing employees for participation in training?
Individual-Level Transfer	**Key Findings:** • Individual characteristics such as motivation, efficacy, learning states and ability and dimensions of personality are important in impacting training transfer • Individual characteristics interact with organisational-level transfer factors to influence the level of transfer • Pre- and post-training self-efficacy are particularly important for interpersonal and soft-skills training

(continued)

Table 6.1 (continued)

Specific Model Component	Key Findings and Research Questions
	Future Research Questions • Researchers need to focus on understanding how individual characteristics influence training transfer sustainment • What role do individual-level transfer issues play in different types of training situations, e.g. blended, MOOCs, virtual, remote? • The role of transfer in linking individual learning and firm outcomes not well understood with major gaps in knowledge • How do changes in motivation, self-efficacy and learning states influence transfer over time?
Organisational-Level Transfer	**Key Findings:** • Learning transfer climate and work environment supports are important for the level of transfer and generalise across multiple types of training and organisational contexts • Supervisory and peer support are particularly important proximate predictors of the transfer of learning **Future Research Questions** • We have a limited knowledge base concerning the impact of organisational-level factors on training transfer over time • Scholars need to investigate the moderating role of organisation-level transfer factors on the relationship between individual learning and human resource outcomes • How, for example, do organisational-level transfer factors act as emergent enablers in influencing human resource outcomes? • What is the most effective combination of interventions to facilitate transfer? • What types of organisational supports are appropriate at different stages of the transfer process? • How do different types of organisational support for transfer impact transfer over time?
Human Capital Resources	**Key Findings:** • Investments in training lead to important human capital resource outcomes for organisations • Training leads to ability, motivation and opportunity-focused human capital resource outcomes

(continued)

Table 6.1 (continued)

Specific Model Component	Key Findings and Research Questions
	• Individual and organisational transfer factors should predict human capital resource outcomes **Future Research Questions** • We lack important insights concerning how individual-level learning translates to organisational-level human capital resources • What dimensions of individual learning outcomes best explain ability versus motivation versus opportunity human capital outcomes? • What is the impact of individual and organisational transfer factors via emergence enablers on human capital resource outcomes?
Emergence Enablers	**Key Findings:** • The research base on emergence enablers in the context of explaining training effectiveness is nascent with the primary focus on cognitive and affective emergence enablers • Researchers have investigated a variety of potential emergence enablers in the context of training effectiveness but not theorised them as emergent phenomenon **Future Research Questions** • What is the relative importance of the different categories of emergent enablers in influencing the extent to which human capital resource outcomes lead to firm operational performance outcomes? • There is significant scope to understand the influence of behavioural emergent enablers such as organisational learning processes, knowledge sharing and hiding and team learning processes • How do emergent enablers influence the long-term impact of human capital resources on firm operational outcomes?
Operational Outcomes	**Key Findings:** • Investments in training lead through a complex sequence, to a variety of firm operational outcomes including productivity, innovation and customer service as well as negative outcomes such as employee turnover • There is some evidence revealing a positive relationship between human capital resource outcomes and firm operational outcomes

(continued)

Table 6.1 (continued)

Specific Model Component	Key Findings and Research Questions
	Future Research Questions • Research must begin to engage with the longitudinal investigation of the determinants of firm operational outcomes • Researches need to better understand the relationships between different operational outcomes and financial outcomes • What is the time lag between the realisation of human capital resource outcomes and firm operational outcomes?
Financial Outcomes	**Key Findings:** • Financial outcomes represent the most important training effectiveness criterion for many organisations • Firm operational outcomes are linked to financial outcomes • Training leads to different types of financial outcomes including sales growth, profitability, market performance and ROE/ROA **Future Research Questions** • How, for example, do financial performance outcomes influence future investment in training? • Researchers need to broaden the scope of outcomes they investigate and more beyond financial to consider social performance • There is a major need to understand the time lag between investment in training and financial performance

individual level in focus, whereas organisational-level human capital refers to the aggregate accumulation of individual human capital that can be combined to create value for the organisation. This therefore, represents a major ambiguity within the literature. Therefore, future research must address this problem.

Future research also needs to isolate the impacts of training and identify whether it is a result of increases in skills and competencies or it is related to attitudinal, affect or motivational components. For example, the AMO proposes that the impact of training or performance will occur primarily through motivation rather than abilities/competencies (Gong et al. 2009). However, while researchers have begun to investigate this possibility, a recent meta-analysis by Garavan et al. (2020) reveals that affect/motivation characteristics are a stronger mediator of the training—organisational performance link than human capital. Therefore, future research should more effectively engage with both of these potential paths as well as also investigating the opportunity component of the AMO model. In particular, it would be important and valuable to investigate the relative value of ability versus motivation versus opportunity in explaining the training—organisational performance link.

6.2.2 The Role of Emergence Enablers

A second critical gap in the literature concerns the investigation of the factors that facilitate the emergence of employee human capital to the organisational level. Kozlowski and Klein (2000) conceptualised these emergent phenomenon as residing in employee cognition, affect and behaviour that become a collective phenomenon. However, in the context of training effectiveness, we have very few insights into the emergence enablers. The theory argues that where the emergence enablers are weak or non-existent, then there is significant less likelihood that individual KSAs will emerge to create organisational human capital that can be mobilised by the organisation for performance. The emergence concept envisages some sort of synergistic effect and organisational-level human capital becomes something more than the aggregation of individual human capital.

Training researchers have, to date, not engaged with how emergence enablers such as knowledge sharing and transfer and collective learning processes act as emergence enablers. In addition to what extent do dimensions such as climate, culture, trust and leadership act as emergence enablers. For example, it is likely that these enablers will contribute to better combinations of human capital, increased organisational agility and adaptability and ambidexterity. In the context of training and firm performance, these emergence enablers will play an important role in moderating the impacts of individual KSAs on unit level or organisation human capital.

6.2.3 Mediating Mechanisms and Boundary Conditions

The model proposed in this monograph to explain training effectiveness highlights the important role of mediating mechanisms. While we have specified a number of these, there are other mediators that are not included in the model. A notable feature of existing research is the lack of attention to mediators generally and the lack of replication of mediators already used. Foremost in terms of the study of mediators is the investigation of supervisory characteristics, team learning processes (Lin and Peng 2010) and co-worker productivity (Bienstock et al. 2003). In addition, there is a need to investigate team characteristics such as team potency (Guzzo et al. 1993), supportive team climate (Ehrhart and Naumann 2004), team learning orientation (Porter 2005), relational social capital within the team (Podsakoff et al. 1997) and interdependencies between team members (Podsakoff and MacKenzie 1994). At the organisational level, there is significant scope to explore issues such as knowledge integration (Collins and Smith 2006), organisational ambidexterity (Patel et al. 2013) and adaptive capability (Wei and Wang 2010).

In terms of boundary conditions or moderators, researchers need to engage with how training design at multiple levels of analysis. Sitzmann and Weinhardt (2015) highlight both macro and micro dimensions of training design that are important. Examples of macro-level moderators include: (a) decisions about what training should be offered; (b) the amount of financial resources provided for training; (c) the types of instruction to be used and (d) the prioritisation of one type of training over another. Examples of micro-level training design characteristics include the way in which the training programmes is framed, how it links to strategic initiatives and the level of support available for training within the team.

There is also a need to investigate other supervisory, team, job/task and organisational characteristics as moderators. Examples of job characteristics that are potentially relevant as moderators include perceived job autonomy, task variety, independence and ambiguity (Podsakoff et al. 2009). Organisational-level moderators that are potentially relevant include organisational formalisation, competitive behaviours, uncertainty, nature of the production processes and trade union membership (Murray and Raffaele 1997). Team characteristics may also act as moderators, such as team cohesion (Chang et al. 2014), team-based learning activities (Peccei and Van de Voorde 2016), types of leadership (Jiang and Men 2015) and quality of relationships with employees (Podsakoff et al. 2014).

6.3 Recommendations for Research Design

6.3.1 Using More Rigorous Research Designs and Capturing Context

An important insight to emerge from our review of the literature on training effectiveness concerns the quality of the research designs used. Quantitative research is the dominant approach within the field with very few qualitative or mixed method studies. In terms of the use of quantitative research, the general conclusion is that these methods are weak. Many of the studies we reviewed suffer from common method issues and a preponderance of cross-sectional designs. There is an absence of longitudinal studies that help researchers to develop insights about the long-term impact of training. The over-reliance in single source, cross-sectional surveys does not generate the types of results that enable strong conclusions to be drawn about training effectiveness.

Another important issue concerns the absence of contextual awareness in the training effectiveness literature. Organisations differ in terms of characteristics, therefore training effectiveness is context dependent. Scholars need to investigate multiple levels of context, including national and organisational. In particular, researchers need to investigate the impact of organisational context on training effectiveness, the comparison of different organisational contexts and studies in different sectors and industries.

6.3.2 Gathering Data from Multiple Stakeholders or Organisational Actors

Studies of training effectiveness need to gather data from multiple actors or stakeholders in organisations. The majority of studies within the field rely on data from employees who have undertaken training. Very few studies gather data from immediate supervisors, managers and senior managers. This weakness is problematic because each stakeholder or actor may have a different perspective on training outcomes. We also recommend that researchers should make greater use of archival data to measure both training and its outcomes (Garavan et al. 2019). Training records bring some objectivity to the study design, however, it is also important to acknowledge their weaknesses. Small firms may not gather and maintain accurate training records (Nolan and Garavan 2016). However, archival data could potentially be combined with employee and manager self-reports, thus providing researchers with better insights into the coverage and extensiveness of training within an organisation.

6.3.3 Addressing Causality and Reverse Causality

The pursuit of causality remains the great unrelated goal in training effectiveness research (Martin et al. 2020). The research designs currently used are not sufficiently robust to make inferences about causality and reverse causality. Both Garavan et al. (2019) and Martin et al. (2020) highlight particular issues that need to be addressed. These include sample representation, the use of control conditions, condition randomisation and independence, temporal designs and author involvement. In reality, it will be difficult to achieve all of these conditions in one study. However, it is important that researchers start out with the requirement to utilise strong research designs and move away from cross-sectional studies and relatively easy to conduct research.

6.4 Implications for Practice

The model explicated in this monograph has a number of important implications for practice. The review of the relevant literature reveals that training is an important organisational activity and that there are many factors that explain its effectiveness. The model we proposed indicates that the context to which training is effective depends on a multiplicity of environmental, organisational, individual and training design inputs as well as elements related to the delivery, implementation and transfer of the learning. We provide a summary of our recommendations for practice related to each component of the model in Table 6.2.

The model suggests that L&D practitioners need to give careful consideration to the outcomes they which to achieve from training and how it links with the strategic goals of the organisation. During the stage of making a proposal for investment in training, L&D practitioners need to ask a number of important questions:

- Who are the most important stakeholders or actors?
- What training effectiveness outcomes are they prioritising and seeking to obtain?
- Is the focus of the training programme on single or multiple outcomes?
- Are some training outcomes more important than others?

Where L&D practitioners have clarity on these questions, then they are more likely going to realise important individual and organisational effectiveness outcomes. Consistent with our review of the evidence on what works and does not work in respect of the design of training, the list of recommendations in Table 6.2 has been derived from the various studies we reviewed. We acknowledge that there is no 'one size fits all' and that L&D practitioners will be required to make assessments of their context and evaluate what will work best at a particular time.

Table 6.2 Key L&D organisational practice implications that arise from our model

Key Model Components	Key Practice Implications
Environmental and Organisational Inputs	• Organisations should continually monitor the external environment to identify what external factors are relevant and their implications for training • Give careful consideration as to what business problems can be addressed through training • Organisational leaders play a major role in developing a strong training culture to maximise training effectiveness • Frame organisational training to ensure a clear link with organisational strategies and links with other HR/L&D practices
Individual Trainee Inputs	• Organisations should spend time developing a strong learning goal orientation and provide support to maximise this orientation to achieve training effectiveness • Pay attention to how trainees are selected for training ad factor in individual differences when designing training • Set clear individual expectations for training and revise expectations in real time
Training Design Inputs	• Conduct systematic training needs prior to training • Instructors and trainers play an important role in shaping trainees' reactions to learning and subsequent KSAs learned • The use of online and mobile technologies should be considered not simply from a cost perspective but from how they maximise learning and learning transfer • Utilise multiple methods and approaches during training to enhance learner reactions to learning
Learner Reactions to Training	• Measure training reactions over time to see how they impact training outcomes • Design training evaluations to measure cognitive, effectiveness and satisfaction (including utility) reactions • Collect data on training reactions from participants and their managers—thus getting a more complete view of reactions • Make use of individual reactions to make decisions about future training

(continued)

Table 6.2 (continued)

Key Model Components	Key Practice Implications
Organisational Reactions to Training	• Gain insights into how feedback on particular training programmes influence senior decision-makers' reactions to training generally • Report back positive training reactions to senior management as a strategy to secure resources for training • Utilise course recommendations intention feedback to enhance training participation and engagement
Individual Learning Outcomes	• Focus on measuring objective as well as subjective measures of learning outcomes • Gather data from multiple sources on learning outcomes—trainees, peers and supervisors should provide data on learning outcomes • Measure learning outcomes at different times to capture the dynamics of learning outcomes
Organisational Learning Outcomes	• Utilise marketing and other tools to create important messages about the value of training and the development of a training culture • Utilise dynamic methods to continually monitor changes in learning needs • Gather data and insights on key learning, participant selection and preparation
Individual-Level Transfer	• Implement strategies to enhance the self-regulation of trainees during different types of training situations • Make use of pre-training interventions to maximise the level of training transfer • Measure systematically the effectiveness of transfer over time
Organisational-Level Transfer	• Pay particular attention to the role of immediate supervisors and peers as vital supports for learning transfer • Look at ways to ensure that leaders are available to support training transfer • Make supervisors through performance management processes accountable for the application of knowledge and skill acquired through training

(continued)

Table 6.2 (continued)

Key Model Components	Key Practice Implications
Human Capital Resources	• Organisations should continually measure human capital outcomes such as engagement, job satisfaction and organisational commitment • Understand how opportunities for employee involvement and empowerment impact operational-level outcomes • Make use of data analysis to develop a human capital resources dashboard
Emergence Enablers	• Pay particular attention to emergent enablers when evaluating the effectiveness of training programmes • Consider how factors such as culture, climate and leadership can enhance the translation of individual learning into organisational learning outcomes • Give particular priority to weak emergence enablers and see how they can be strengthened
Operational Outcomes	• Organisations should measure how different training options impact operational outcomes such as productivity and customer service • When making choices about training, organisations should first identify the operational outcomes that are important to them • Organisations should make sure of data analytic capabilities to collect longitudinal data on operational outcomes
Financial Outcomes	• Organisations and L&D practitioners should be realistic about the complexities involved in measuring the bottom-line outcomes of training • Organisations should conduct ROI studies on high-profile training investments and use this data to justify future training investments

6.5 Conclusions

The aim of this monograph was to approach the topic of training effectiveness in a more integrated and dynamic way. In general, we can conclude that the area of training effectiveness in organisations is ripe for further development; however, there is a need for research that links the value change from training to firm performance. We encourage researchers to develop new insights and knowledge based on rigorous research and to share this research with practitioners so that they can build their approach to training based on evidence. The results of our model clearly have a variety of practical implications for the positioning of training, its design and delivery. There is a major need for an evidence-based approach to practise yet the gaps in terms of practitioner priorities and scholarly contribution are considerable.

References

Bienstock, C. C., DeMoranville, C. W., & Smith, R. K. (2003). Organizational citizenship behaviour and service quality. *Journal of Services Marketing, 17*(4), 357–378.

Chang, S., Jia, L., Takeuchi, R., & Cai, Y. (2014). Do high commitment work systems affect creativity? A multilevel combinational approach to employee creativity. *Journal of Applied Psychology, 99*, 665–680.

Collins, C., & Smith, K. (2006). Knowledge exchange and combination: The role of human resource practices in the performance of high-technology firms. *The Academy of Management Journal, 49*(3), 544–560.

Ernhart, M. G., & Naumann, S. E. (2004). Organisational citizens in work groups: A group norms approach. *Journal of Applied Psychology, 89*, 960–974.

Garavan, T. N., Heneghan, S., O'Brien, F., Gubbins, C., Lai, Y., Carbery, R., et al. (2019). L&D professionals in organisations: Much ambition, unfulfilled promise. *European Journal of Training and Development, 44*(1), 1–86.

Garavan, T., McCarthy, A., Lai, Y., Murphy, K., Sheehan, M., & Carbery, R. (2020). Training and organisational performance: A meta-analysis of temporal, institutional, and organisational context moderators. *Human Resource Management Journal*, in-press.

Gong, Y., Huang, J. C., & Farh, J. L. (2009). Employee learning orientation, transformational leadership, and employee creativity: The mediating role of employee self-efficacy. *Academy of Management Journal, 52*(4), 765–778.

Guzzo, R. A., Yost, P. R., Campbell, R. J., & Shea, G. P. (1993). Potency in groups: Articulating a construct. *British Journal of Social Psychology, 32*(1), 87–106.

Jiang, H., & Men, L. R. (2015). Creating an engaged workforce: The impact of authentic leadership, transparent organisational communication, and work-life enrichment. *Communication Research, 44*(2), 225–243.

Kozlowski, S. W. J., & Klein, K. J. (2000). A multilevel approach to theory and research in organizations: Contextual, temporal, and emergent processes. In K. J. Klein & S. W. J. Kozlowski (Eds.), *Multilevel theory, research and methods in organizations: Foundations, extensions, and new directions* (pp. 3–90). San Francisco, CA: Jossey-Bass.

Lin, C. C., & Peng, T. K. (2010). From organisational citizenship to team performance: The mediation of group cohesion and collective efficacy. *Management and Organisation Review, 6*, 55–75.

Martin, R., Hughes, D. J., Epitropaki, O., & Thomas, G. (2020). In pursuit of causality in leadership training research: A review and pragmatic recommendations. *The Leadership Quarterly*, in-press.

Murray, B., & Raffaele, G. C. (1997). Single-site, results-level evaluation of quality awareness training. *Human Resource Development Quarterly, 8*(3), 229–245.

Nolan, C. T., & Garavan, T. (2016). Human resource development in SMEs. *International Journal of Management Reviews, 18*(1), 85–107.

Patel, P. C., Messersmith, J. G., & Lepak, D. P. (2013). Walking the tightrope: An assessment of the relationship between high-performance work systems and organizational ambidexterity. *Academy of Management Journal, 56*(5), 1420–1442.

Peccei, R., & Van de Voorde, K. (2016). The application of the multilevel paradigm in human resource management-outcomes research: Taking stock and going forward. *Journal of Management, 45*(2), 786–818.

Ployhart, R. E., & Moliterno, T. P. (2011). Emergence of the human capital resource: A multi-level model. *The Academy of Management Review, 36*(1), 127–150.

Ployhart, R. E., Nyberg, A. J., Reilly, G., & Maltarich, M. A. (2014). Human capital is dead; long live human capital resources! *Journal of Management, 40*, 371–398.

Podsakoff, N. P., Podsakoff, P. M., Mackenzie, S. B., Maynes, T., & Spoelma, T. (2014). Consequences of unit-level organizational citizenship behaviours: A review and recommendations for future research. *Journal of Organizational Behaviour, 35*(51), 87–119.

Podsakoff, N. P., Whiting, S. W., Podsakoff, P. M., & Blume, B. D. (2009). Individual- and organizational-level consequences of organizational citizenship behaviours: A meta-analysis. *Journal of Applied Psychology, 94*, 122–141.

Podsakoff, P. M., & MacKenzie, S. B. (1994). Organizational citizenship behaviours and sales unit effectiveness. *Journal of Marketing Research, 3*, 351–363.

Podsakoff, P. M., Ahearne, M., & MacKenzie, S. B. (1997). Organizational citizenship behaviour and the quantity and quality of work group performance. *Journal of Applied Psychology, 82*, 262–270.

Porter, C. O. L. H. (2005). Goal orientation: Effects on backing up behaviour, performance, efficacy, and commitment in teams. *Journal of Applied Psychology, 90*, 811–818.

Sitzmann, T., & Weinhardt, J. M. (2015). Training engagement theory: A multilevel perspective on the effectiveness of work-related training. *Journal of Management, 44*(2), 732–756.

Wei, H. L., & Wang, E. T. G. (2010). The strategic value of supply chain visibility: Increasing the ability to reconfigure. *European Journal of Information Systems, 19*, 238–249.

Wright, P. M., & McMahan, G. C. (2011). Exploring human capital: Putting 'human' back into strategic human resource management. *Human Resource Management Journal, 21*, 93–104.

Index

T. N. Garavan et al.
Learning and Development Effectiveness in Organisations,
https://doi.org/10.1007/978-3-030-48900-7

The manufacturer's authorised representative in the EU is Springer Nature Customer Service Centre GmbH, Europaplatz 3, 69115 Heidelberg, Germany. If you have any concerns regarding our products, please contact ProductSafety@springernature.com

Printed and bound by CPI Group (UK) Ltd, Croydon, CR0 4YY
30/09/2026
02225450-0002